N.C. HITCHEN   2V
14-95

Rating Valuation
A Practical Guide

Rating Valuation
A Practical Guide

Frances A S Plimmer, ARICS, ARVA,
F Land Inst

Longman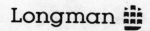

© Longman Group UK Limited 1987

Published by
Longman Group UK Ltd
21–27 Lamb's Conduit Street
London WC1N 3NJ

Associated offices
Australia, Hong Kong, Malaysia, Singapore, USA

British Library Cataloguing in Publication Data

Plimmer, Frances A.S.
  Rating valuation : a practical guide.
  1. Real property tax—Law and legislation
  —England 2. Local taxation—Law and
  legislation—England
  I. Title
  344.2035'42   KD5729

  ISBN 0–85121–320–0

Printed and bound in Great Britain by
Biddles Ltd, Guildford and King's Lynn

This book is dedicated to
William Sterry Evans FAI FIArb
and to the second year students of the
BSc Degree in Urban Estate Management
at the Polytechnic of Wales –
past, present and future.

'In the end, therefore, we are in a world of make-believe.'

per Willmer LJ in *Humber Ltd* v *Jones (VO)*, (1960) 6 RRC 161, 171.

Contents

Contents

Tables

Foreword

Reading recent reports contained in the general and professional press one might be forgiven for thinking that the demise of the whole rating system was at hand—but this is a misleading impression derived from proposals to abolish rates on residential property only. Whatever happens to domestic rates the rating system as applied to all other property looks set to be with us for the forseeable future.

When new valuation lists are about to be prepared it is timely to have a new, up-to-date and comprehensive work from which to get a sound understanding of the basis of rating, its administration, valuation considerations relating to it and relevant legal decisions together with methods of valuation and appeal procedures.

A quick glance at the text of this book will reveal how much there is to know on the subject and although it is not something to read all at once it does give comprehensive cover of the subject and should be of particular interest to the non-specialist professional and those preparing for professional qualifications.

In the interests of completeness of each section of the book there is some overlap of subject matter, but the helpful 'synopsis' and 'checklist' at the beginning and end of each chapter should enable the reader to make references with ease and speed.

This book fills a gap between over simplified publications on rating directed mainly at the domestic scene and the exhaustive reference book.

Philip R V Watkins FRICS
Past President of the Royal Institution of Chartered Surveyors
February 1987

ix

Preface

This book has been written for the non-specialist professional, whether student or practitioner, who needs a practical guide through the principles and practice of valuing property for rating purposes. It is of particular relevance to students of valuation techniques studying for internal or external examinations.

With the decision of the present Conservative government to retain commercial rating, and to phase out domestic rating over a ten year period, apparently from 1990, the future of rating seems certain, if not secure. With this certainty established, it is increasingly important that all ratepayers and their advisers are informed and familiar with the legalities which affect their liability.

The book has been structured around a series of questions: Who pays rates? On what property is rates payable? Are rates paid in all circumstances? Is the occupier always liable? What is the basis on which rates are calculated? What are the valuation techniques used in rating? What are the particular problems relating to the valuation of selected property types? How are the values compiled, maintained and altered? How are rates actually collected?

With the exceptions of Chapter 1 (Rates in context) and Chapter 13 (Administration) each chapter begins with a 'Synopsis' which highlights the relevance of the chapter; and, at the end of each chapter (except Chapters 1, 10 and 13), there is a 'Checklist', providing a brief list of all relevant points covered. These are to guide the reader more easily through the information.

There are available excellent texts which give more detailed consideration to many of the issues dealt with here, and, where such detail is required, reference should be made to the texts mentioned in the Bibliography, and, of course, to relevant statutes and cases.

It has been assumed that the reader has an understanding of the basic principles of valuation, enabling the text to show how these basic principles are adapted for rating purposes.

The legislation covered in this book is applicable only to England and Wales (not to Scotland or Northern Ireland) and every effort has been made to ensure that it is correct as at 1 December 1986.

I am indebted to my family, colleagues and friends for their support and encouragement, and especially to Mr Philip Watkins for kindly agreeing to write the Foreword, to Philip Cooper, Christine Llewellyn, Barbara Richardson, Hilda Sterry-Evans, Martyn Williams and to the Chief Valuer's Office, with special thanks to Stuart Gronow for help in structuring and presenting the text.

FASP
February 1987

Table of Cases

References in the tables are to paragraph numbers.

xiii

Table of Statutes

Table of Statutory Instruments

Abbreviations

In addition to the usual abbreviations to be found in published texts, the following have been adopted.

GRA 1967   General Rate Act 1967
The 1967 Act   General Rate Act 1967
LGPLA 1980   Local Government Planning and Land Act 1980
The 1980 Act   Local Government Planning and Land Act 1980
VO   Valuation officer
AP   Aggrieved person
LVC   Local valuation court
RCA   Reduced covered area
EFA   Effective floor area

Author's note

The law of rating stems from the provisions of the General Rate Act 1967 as amended and supplemented by the various subsequent statutes.

References to statutes are to the General Rate Act 1967 unless the contrary is stated.

Chapter 1

Rates in context

What are rates?

1.1 Rates, or more specifically the general rate, are a *local tax* based on the value of property, paid by local people to a local authority, which is responsible for providing services within the locality.

1.2 Although there are other 'rates' (eg water rate, sea defence rate, garden rate etc), it is the *general rate* which will be meant by the term 'rate'.

1.3 The general rate is the tax *levied by the local (rating) authority* on the ratepayers in its area.

1.4 The general rate is *based on the value of property* and is a tax on the occupation of property.

1.5 Rates originated in the form of a nationwide local property tax as a result of the Poor Relief Act 1601. Sometimes called the Statute of Elizabeth, the objective of the Act was to provide a welfare system for '. . . the necessary relief of the lame, impotent, old, blind and such other among them, being poor and not able to work, and also for the putting out of such children to be apprentices . . .'.

1.6 The administration was carried out by the Overseers of the Poor and the finance came from 'taxation' levied on '. . . every inhabitant, parson, vicar and other, and . . . every occupier of lands, houses, tithes . . . coal mines or saleable underwoods in the said parish . . .'.

1.7 Later the role of administration passed from Overseers of the Poor to local authorities which were authorised to use the money raised for their many and varied responsibilities (see Appendix 1: History of rating).

1

Who pays rates?

1.8   Rates are paid by *occupiers* of property. The liability to pay rates is based on the occupation of property, not on ownership.

1.9   Owners will pay rates on property they own and occupy, but they will pay rates only because they are occupiers. Very rarely will owners pay rates in their capacity as owners, and these are exceptional cases (see Chapter 6: Rating of owners).

1.10   In order to be liable for rates, an occupier must be in *rateable occupation* of premises.

1.11   Rateable occupation is strictly defined (Chapter 2: Rateable occupation). However, not all occupiers pay rates.

1.12   Tenants pay rates, either directly to the local authority or to their landlord together with rent. The landlord will pass the rates money on to the local authority.

1.13   Lodgers are unlikely to pay rates; they are unlikely to fulfil the requirements of rateable occupation, since they normally occupy together with the owner or tenant who will be the ratepayer. Squatters are likely to pay rates, or at least to be liable for rates, because they will probably conform to the definition of a rateable occupier (see Chapter 2).

1.14   In addition, there are numerous exemptions and reliefs available under specific circumstances (see Chapter 5: Exemptions and reliefs).

1.15   Originally, rates were paid by '. . . every inhabitant, parson, vicar and other, and . . . every occupier of lands, houses, tithes . . . coal mines or saleable underwoods in the said parish . . .'.

1.16   Over the years, 'inhabitants . . .' etc have been exempted liability to rates, leaving only the occupier responsible for the tax.

Who spends the rates?

1.17   Rates are a local tax paid by local occupiers for local services. They are paid to a special kind of local authority, a *rating authority*.

1.18   Not all local authorities are rating authorities, so not all local authorities are entitled to levy rates.

1.19   Within the local government system, *rating authorities* are the district councils and borough councils (with two additional authorities in the Inner and Middle Temples), and only these can levy rates.

1.20   Other local authorities inform the rating authority how much money they require from the rates and the rating authority includes an extra rate in the £ for the other local authorities' requirements. This is called 'precepting'.

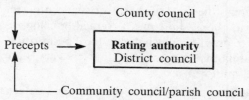

1.21 In any one county, there are likely to be several district councils (rating authorities); however, there are not always community councils (in Wales) or parish councils (in England), so that any county council should precept on several district councils (rating authorities), but several community or parish councils will precept on the same district council (rating authority).

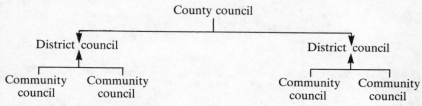

1.22 At each level, local authorities are responsible for certain services within the locality.

What are rates used for?

1.23 Rates are now just one of more than half a dozen sources of income for a local authority and, together with other sources of income, finance local *services* which the local authorities have a statutory obligation to provide, as follows:

	Percentages of funds applied
Education	33
Council housing	25
Environmental services (refuse collection, parks, planning etc)	13
Social services (meals on wheels etc)	7.5
Police	10
Roads	8.5
Others (eg fire service, bus service, libraries, consumer protection)	3

(Source: *Local Government Gross Expenditure England 1984/85*, Annex A: 'Paying for local government', January 1986)

1.24   Local authorities can spend money only as authorised by Act of Parliament, and the law requires that they provide the majority of the services for which they are responsible. However, local authorities have freedom to determine the *level* of those services within their area, and it is this freedom to choose how much council housing, road facilities, social services etc to provide, which makes local authorities so important to the local inhabitants, and the freedom to vary their income so important to local authorities.

1.25   Most of the local authorities' income is fixed externally, beyond the control of the authorities themselves.

1.26   In 1984/85 local authorities' income of £39 billion was produced from the following sources:

Government grants and subsidies		42%
Rates: non-domestic	17%	
domestic	11%	28%
Sales, fees and charges		9%
Rents		4%
Capital receipts		6%
Borrowing		6%
Other		5%

(Source: *Sources of Local Government Income England 1984/85*, Annex A: 'Paying for local government', January 1986)

1.27   *Government grants* are controlled by central government, and there has been strong central government pressure to control and reduce local spending. Originally, the grant system was introduced to reduce the level of rates on relatively poor rural areas, and to allow their authorities to provide a level of services comparable to that provided by the relatively rich urban areas. However, recently they have become a tool for controlling the national economy (see 1.41–2).

1.28   *Charges* for services tend to be fixed at or near a break-even point and there is no room for flexibility. This is also true of new *borrowing*, which is expensive and unpopular. The **sale of assets** produces little income and reduces capital assets.

1.29   Of these sources of income only rates give local authorities any degree of flexibility, and therefore allow flexibility in the level of services which they provide.

How are rates fixed?

1.30   **Rates paid equal rate in the pound multiplied by rateable value.**

1.31   The *rate in the pound* is fixed by the rating authority, by resolution, for a rate period of twelve months (a financial year) and is always given in terms of a penny rate, eg 205.7p.

1.32 The *rateable value* is a value attached to the property on which rates are levied.

1.33 So, for any ratepayer who knows the rateable value of his property and the rate in the pound fixed by the rating authority, the calculation of his *rate liability* for the rate period is simple, eg:

Rate in the £205.7p × £380 rateable value
= rates payable of £781.66

1.34 Although the rate liability is fixed for twelve months, rates are *demanded* (in advance) at six-monthly intervals, on 1 April and 1 October in any year. Generally they may be paid in ten monthly instalments over a year.

1.35 All rateable values for any given rating area appear in the *valuation list* for that area. Included in the valuation list is the total of all rateable values for that rating area, so that whenever the rating authority needs to calculate the rate in the pound, it first estimates how much rates are required from all the ratepayers and then:

$$\frac{\text{Rates required to be paid}}{\text{Total rateable value of the area}} = \text{Rate in the £}$$

1.36 For example, assume that £2,839,890 is required from rate revenue and that the total rateable value of the rating area is £1,380,598 then:

$$\frac{£2,839,890}{£1,380,598} = 205.7p$$

so the rate in the pound necessary to achieve the required income level is 205.7p.

1.37 Prior to the imposition of *rate-capping* which effectively limits the increases in the rate in the pound to the percentage permitted by central government, the flexibility of rates could be demonstrated by the fact that the only control over such increases was that of the ratepayers, who by publicity and the ballot box could control the local authorities' income from the rates.

1.38 In principle, therefore, rates can be adjusted to make up any shortfall between a local authority's desired expenditure and the income from other fixed sources.

1.39 Bear in mind, however, that only adults resident in the parish who have their names on the electoral register have the **right to vote** in local authority elections, and not all these are ratepayers. Similarly, a ratepayer who occupies business premises in one parish but lives in another parish will not have a vote in the parish where his business premises are located. Those who pay rates on business premises have no right to vote in local elections unless able to vote as residential occupiers; this situation will only arise if both home and business are in the same electoral area.

1.40 However, the government has imposed a new statutory duty on local authorities to **consult** with representatives of the **business community** before fixing their rate poundages or precepts, and this should go some way towards pacifying commercial ratepayers who perceive rates as a crushing burden over which they have no electoral control.

1.41 In addition, in its attempt to **control the national economy**, the government has found a way of limiting the power of local authorities to increase the level of rates which they levy.

1.42 Over the years of the 1979–87 Conservative government, economic stringencies have been imposed at all levels of government. The autonomy of local government to spend its money as it thinks fit within its own locality, without regard for national economic policy, has been severely restricted by the imposition of **rate-capping** under the Rates Act 1984.

1.43 Rate-capping involves the Secretary of State for the Environment imposing limits on the increases in expenditure which local authorities can make in any financial year. The failure of the local authority to observe these limits will result in cuts in the rate support grant to that authority.

How are valuers involved?

1.44 As explained, rates paid equals rate in the pound multiplied by rateable value.

1.45 The rate in the pound is fixed by the rating authority for each rate period (financial year).

1.46 However, the **rateable value** is a value of property and a valuer is involved in fixing that value. The rateable value is strictly defined in statute and case law (Chapters 7 and 8: Basis and Principles of assessment).

1.47 All **methods of valuation** are used to produce rateable values within the law established by statute and case law (Chapters 9 and 10: Methods of valuation and Valuation of selected property types).

1.48 Having fixed a rateable value, it may be necessary to *establish*, *challenge* or *defend* that value. (Chapters 11 and 12: The valuation list, and Proposals and appeals). Again, a valuer's skill is required for this. Even if the challenge is on legal grounds, the effect of the law may be to change the value of the property and, in practice, a valuer may be both *expert witness* and *advocate* in a court case.

1.49 However, knowledge of valuation techniques and the values within the locality are not sufficient to assess a rateable value. A valuer will need to know rating legal principles and to apply his valuation skills within those principles.

1.50 The principles are complex, but relatively well established. Many of the principles were the result of case law decisions and only rarely has statute interfered to clarify or amend the law.

1.51 However, despite all the law, both statute and case law, which exists to fix a rateable value, this is only a *means to an end*—a system whereby revenue can be raised for local expenditure—ie a *local property tax*.

1.52 Rates have been in existence in substantially the same form for centuries, and the system is often bitterly criticised. It is *not a perfect system*, and in Appendix 2 there is a consideration of the *advantages* and *disadvantages* of rates as a revenue-raising system (a local property tax), and in Appendix 3 consideration is given to the future of rating, in so far as it can be seen to date.

1.53 The ultimate decision on the future of rates is, of course, made by central government and is, therefore, the result of a *political* choice, taking into account factors over and above the rating system itself.

Chapter 2

Rateable occupation

Synopsis

2.1 'The occupier, not the land, is rateable; but the occupier is rateable in respect of the land which he occupies.' (*Westminster City Council v Southern Rail Co Ltd* (1936).)

2.2 Rates are an occupiers' tax. If there is no occupier, there are no rates. Occupation means a factual possession of land, not a legal possession. Title is, therefore, irrelevant.

2.3 There are four elements of rateable occupation:

(a) actual possession, ie a factual holding or use made of the land;
(b) exclusive occupation, ie the ability to exclude all others from using the land in the same way; or the ability to control the use of land by others who use the land in the same way;
(c) beneficial occupation, ie the occupation of the land must be of value;
(d) permanence, ie a sufficient length of occupation to become liable to a rate.

2.4 For rateable occupation, all four elements must be present.

Occupation

2.5 Under the Poor Relief Act 1601, a rate was to be paid by every inhabitant and every occupier of lands, houses, coal mines or saleable underwoods in the parish.

2.6 Liability to pay rates is now found in s 16 GRA 1967 which states that '. . . every *oocupier* of property . . . shall be liable to be assessed to rates in respect of . . . that property . . .'.

2.7 Although it is often said that a particular property is rateable, this is not strictly true. It is the *occupier* who is rateable in respect of his occupation of property.

2.8   On this basis, if there is no occupier, there is no liability to rates (but see Chapter 6).

2.9   There is no statutory definition of either 'occupier' or 'occupation'. However, in *Laing (John) & Son Ltd* v *Kingswood Assessment Area Assessment Committee* (1949) the Court of Appeal recognised *four essential elements of rateable occupation*:

  (a) actual possession;
  (b) exclusive occupation;
  (c) beneficial occupation;
  (d) sufficient degree of permanence.

2.10   Although the four essential elements were recognised in 1949, the law on rateable occupation was developed over the centuries by judicial decisions. Some of the cases which comprise and illustrate the law may deal with matters which are not important or relevant today. Nevertheless, the decisions were milestones of their time and their principles still hold good.

Ownership and possession distinguished

2.11   It has proved very difficult to give a concise definition of 'occupation' for rating purposes. The most cited definition is that in *R* v *St Pancras Assessment Committee* (1877):

> *Occupation includes possession* as its primary element, *but it also includes something more*. Legal possession does not of itself constitute an occupation. The owner of a vacant house is in possession, and may maintain trespass against anyone who invades it, but as long as he leaves it vacant he is not rateable for it as an occupier. If, however, he furnishes it, and keeps it ready for habitation whenever he pleases to go to it, he is an occupier, though he may not reside in it one day in a year.
>
> On the other hand, a person who, without having any title, takes actual possession of a house or piece of land, whether by leave of the owner or against his will, is the occupier of it.

2.12   Thus, the courts made a clear distinction between legal possession which does not give rise to liability to pay rates, and actual possession which does.

2.13   *Legal possession* means legal title to use land and is very much a matter of law. Legal possession alone will not create liability to pay rates.

2.14 *Actual possession* means the physical presence of the occupier on the land or the acts by which he makes use of or controls the land. The existence of actual possession is a matter of fact and, in order for someone to be rated as an occupier, he must be in actual possession.

2.15 It follows from this that, if liability to pay rates is based on the fact of actual possession, the *legal title of the 'occupier' becomes irrelevant* in determining that liability.

2.16 Thus, a trespasser could be a rateable occupier and, therefore, liable to rates provided he had actual possession.

2.17 The only occasion when *title* may be considered in determining rateable occupation occurs when someone's use of land may be consistent with either a right to full occupation or with the existence of a mere licence.

2.18 The consideration of title cannot be used to reduce liability (so that if the owner of an easement over land has such an extensive use of that land so that he effectively occupies it, he cannot use the easement title as an excuse to deny occupation and thereby prevent rateability). However, title may be considered to decide liability when a person's use of land, which results from an easement or licence, does not involve complete possession or the use is ambiguous.

2.19 Where *owners* have any use at all of land, they are rateable occupiers of it, unless it can be shown that someone else actually occupies it.

2.20 But the owner of land or buildings who does not use it in any way is not rateable for it because, although he has legal possession, he is not in actual possession.

Actual possession

2.21 Actual possession means the physical presence of the occupier on the land, or the *acts by which he makes use of or controls the land*. The existence of actual possession is a matter of fact and, in order for someone to be rated as an occupier, he must be in actual possession.

2.22 An *intention* to occupy property is insufficient to create rateable occupation (*Associated Cinema Properties Ltd* v *Hampstead Borough Council* (1944)).

2.23 Intention is relevant only when it goes to show present occupation and user.

2.24 There must be some act of user, together with intention, for actual possession to exist.

2.25 However, it is important to remember that the *nature of occupation necessarily varies with the nature of the rateable subject matter*, and this may be relevant, for example, if the nature of the property involves periods when the property is not in use.

2.26 In the case of non-domestic property which is not obviously in use, it is necessary to establish whether the owner is getting the use of the property which he intended to have when he purchased or rented it. If he is, then he is also in actual possession and, therefore, rateable (*Liverpool Corporation* v *Chorley Union* (1913)).

2.27 Although land may be used even though no positive acts are carried out with regard to it, for occupation to arise something *must actually be done on the land*—either on the whole or on a part in respect of the whole.

2.28 Occupation can result even from a *slight use* of land (*Liverpool Corporation* v *Chorley Union* (1913)).

2.29 In the days before 1929, when agricultural land was rated, land used for growing crops etc was rateable, even though no one set foot on it for months, or even years.

2.30 Because rates are based on an annual tenancy (see Chapter 7), cases arose where occupation did not in fact last twelve months. Among these were *Mayor etc of Southend-on-Sea* v *White* (1900) concerning a seaside shop, and *Gage* v *Wren* (1903) concerning a seaside lodging house.

2.31 Where *occupation is seasonal*, for example premises are closed during winter months, occupiers are still rateable during the whole year.

2.32 This is not as unreasonable as it may at first appear. Rates paid are based on the rateable value, which is an annual rental value of a property, determined according to a statutory definition (see Chapter 7). If a property is only profitable for part of the year, the rent paid is based on that fact and, presumably, is lower than if profit lasted twelve months. If rates are based on this lower rent, the seasonal profitability of the occupation has been taken into account.

2.33 There are some *acts which do not amount to occupation* if carried out by an owner, for example acts carried out purely as a result of ownership such as keeping an empty house weather-tight. Also, buildings in the course of construction or alteration are not rateable because there can be no occupier within the meaning of ss 16 and 79(2)(*a*).

2.34 *Parts of a building site* may, however, be so used as to be rateable in the occupation of the builders, eg builders' huts occupied in one location for a sufficient length of time have been held to be rateable (see 2.68).

2.35 When *structural alterations* are made to a building which continues to be rateable, the works may constitute grounds for a reduction in the assessment (see Chapter 8).

Exclusive occupation

2.36 Exclusive occupation involves the use of land by someone who, by the nature of the occupation, *can exclude everyone else from using the land in the same way*.

2.37 There are occasions when separate occupations will exist in respect of the same land. Thus, where two (or more) people use the same land, but for different purposes, if each is able to exclude the other from using the land in the same way, each will have exclusive occupation and be rateable for the different use each makes of the land (*Holywell Union* v *Halkyn District Mines Drainage Co* (1895) and *Ryan Industrial Fuels Ltd* v *Morgan (VO)* (1965)).

2.38 *Title is irrelevant* in determining rateable occupation (see 2.15) but it may be considered where the facts are ambiguous. In such a case there is a *presumption* that *the owner who has any use of his land is the occupier*, until it is shown that occupation is in the hands of another.

2.39 The presumption is used in cases of a slight user in which reference to title is necessary to establish occupation.

2.40 Someone without title to the exclusive occupation of land may be the rateable occupier if his *occupation is exclusive in fact*. If the nature of the use he makes of the land is such that others are excluded from using it in the same way, he will (if the other ingredients of rateable occupation are satisfied) be rateable (*Westminster City Council* v *Southern Rail Co Ltd* (1936)).

2.41 Where there are *two persons* who have a similar use of land so that neither is able to exclude the other from using the land in the same way the other does, the occupation which is rateable is the *paramount occupation*, ie the rateable occupier will be able to *control the use* made of the premises by the other.

2.42 In *Westminster City Council* v *Southern Rail Co Ltd* (1936) the principles to be applied in determining paramount occupation were laid down.

2.43 Where persons occupy parts of a larger hereditament and the owner is also in occupation, he is presumed to retain control of the occupied parts and to be in paramount occupation and, thus, in rateable occupation. If the owner retains no control over the use made of the parts occupied by others, the occupiers of the various parts will be treated as in rateable occupation of the parts.

2.44 An occupying owner will be presumed to be in control of parts occupied by another unless he can prove otherwise (*Helman* v *Horsham and Worthing Area Assessment Committee* (1949)).

2.45 Similarly, control over access to the occupied premises without control over their use will not create rateable occupation, and the imposition of regulations and/or byelaws over the use of premises will not prevent the rateability of the occupier on whom these are imposed if it can be shown that they are in the nature of restrictive covenants (*Westminster City Council* v *Southern Rail Co Ltd* (1936)).

2.46 Generally, it is accepted that a *lodger* is not rateable, while the *tenant* of a flat is rateable, because although a lodger is said to occupy a room, his tenancy does not usually amount to what rating law recognises as occupation. A lodger's room consists of part of a larger building but, in most cases, the lodger holds subject to the general control which the landlord exercises over the whole property, including the room let to the lodger.

2.47 The occupation by a tenant of a flat will be rateable because, although he occupies part of a larger building, the use of the flat is not subject to the control of his landlord.

2.48 *Control* means control exercised over the use of the premises while the tenancy lasts, not just the right to terminate the tenancy. The right to say *how* a tenant shall use a landlord's property is not the same as the right to say for *how long* the tenant shall use it.

2.49 The distinction between a lodger (who is not a rateable occupier) and a tenant (who may be a rateable occupier) was made in *Bradley* v *Bayliss* (1881), a case concerning parliamentary franchise, but referred to in rating law to distinguish a lodger from a tenant:

> Where the owner of the house does not let the whole of it, but retains a part for his own use, and resides there, and does not let out the passages and staircases to the outer door but only lets to the tenants the right of ingress and egress; and where the owner retains the control over the staircases and passages to the outer doors—that is, where he retains a right to interfere, and to turn out trespassers and the like—there I consider that the landlord is the occupying tenant of the house, and the inmate . . . is a lodger.

That is one extreme case. Again, where the landlord lets out the whole of the house in separate apartments, . . . so as to demise the passages, reserving simply to each inmate of the upper floors the right of ingress and egress over the lower passages, parting altogether with the whole legal ownership, and retaining no control over the house, there . . . the inmates are occupying tenants, and are rateable as such. That is another extreme case. There are a great number of intermediate cases . . .

Beneficial occupation

2.50 The third requirement of rateable occupation is beneficial occupation, which means that the occupation should be *of value* to the occupier, and for which a tenant would give a *rent* which is greater than the outgoings on the property (*LCC* v *Erith and West Ham* (1893)). It does not mean that the occupation should be profitable.

2.51 In the case of private property, if any profit made is totally absorbed by the agreed rent to the landlord, the tenant is in beneficial occupation and, therefore, rateable.

2.52 However, with the correct interpretation of beneficial occupation as being of value to an occupier, premises which cannot be run profitably or where the occupiers, such as a charitable organisation, make no profit, may still be in beneficial occupation.

2.53 The test in rateability is not whether the property will produce a profit, but whether it will produce a *rent*.

2.54 Even if the actual occupier pays no rent, it is necessary to consider whether the property is capable of commanding a rent from anyone else (*West Bromwich School Board* v *West Bromwich Overseers* (1884)).

2.55 Alternatively, where property is owner-occupied, consider whether, if the property were owned by another, the actual owner-occupier would be prepared to pay a rent to occupy the premises. If so, the occupation of that property is beneficial. This applies particularly to occupiers with a *statutory duty* to perform, for which purpose they occupy property and where there is no rival demand from anyone else (*Mayor etc of Burton-upon-Trent* v *Burton-upon-Trent Union* (1889)).

2.56 Land for which no rent would be paid is said to be *struck with sterility*. Land dedicated to the public as a highway is 'struck with sterility' because, while the dedication lasts and the public has such extensive rights of user over it, no tenant would pay rent for it. (The 'public' cannot be a rateable occupier, *Lambeth Overseers* v *LCC* (1897).)

2.57 Public parks and recreation grounds subject to extensive public rights of user are not in the beneficial occupation of the local authority which owns and maintains them (*Lambeth Overseers* v *LCC* (1897), also called the *Brockwell Park* case) (see Chapter 5).

2.58 The actual use of such property must, in fact, give the public free and unrestricted use of the property. This does not prevent the implementation of proper regulations designed to protect the public's enjoyment of the land's amenities, as contrasted with restrictions designed 'not merely to provide amenities for the public but also to make a revenue' (*North Riding of Yorkshire County Valuation Committee* v *Redcar Corporation* (1943)).

2.59 The lack of beneficial occupation exists not only for the land directly subject to the public rights, but also to any necessary ancillary of the property, eg a refreshment pavilion in a park (*Sheffield Corporation* v *Tranter (VO)* (1957)).

2.60 It is a question of fact and degree whether the part in question is to be treated as an ancillary of the main property or whether the part has been so carved out as to acquire a distinct status of its own which renders it liable to be rated separately (see Chapter 4).

2.61 If a profit is made in the course of managing land for the benefit of the public, it would be very difficult, if not impossible, to establish a right to exemption from rates on the grounds of lack of beneficial occupation, since the rights of the public would not have exhausted the value of land. The fact that profit is actually made will be strong, if not conclusive, evidence of rateability (*North Riding of Yorkshire County Valuation Committee* v *Redcar Corporation* (1943)).

2.62 However, a profit on part only of a public recreation ground will not justify the separate rating of that part, if it is merely ancillary to the whole and the whole shows no prospect of producing a profit (*Sheffield Corporation* v *Tranter (VO)* (1957)).

2.63 If land is held on trust for the use of a class of person which is less than the public in extent, the owners will be the rateable occupier (*Hyde Corporation* v *Wilkes (VO) and Ashton Trustees* (1958)).

2.64 Provided there is actual occupation, ie acts of user, and the occupation is exclusive, the fact that the hereditament may not be used to the full by the occupier is irrelevant. Rateability can only be avoided by abandoning the use of the property altogether.

2.65 There are certain acts which do not constitute beneficial occupation. Although keeping furniture in a house not otherwise used amounts to beneficial occupation (*Staley* v *Castleton Overseers* (1864)), where furniture or goods are left behind when premises are vacated solely because it is not worth removing them, this does not amount to beneficial occupation (*LCC* v *Hackney Borough Council* (1928)).

Permanent occupation

2.66 To be rateable, occupation must have a sufficient degree of permanence, and the courts will consider not only the *length* of the occupation but its *character* as well.

2.67 In *R* v *St Pancras Assessment Committee* (1877) it was held that, because the rate is fixed for a period of months, it would be absurd to make liable for rates a person who comes into a parish intending to remain there a few days or a week only. Thus, a transient, temporary holding of land is not enough to make the occupier rateable.

2.68 Builders' huts in position for more than a year have been held to be rateable. An occupation can be permanent even though the structure or chattel which is the means of occupation is removable on notice. It may be that permanent signifies no more than *continuous*, as opposed to intermittent, *physical possession of the soil* (*LCC* v *Wilkins (VO)* (1957)).

2.69 Liability to have an occupation terminated by notice or at will does not prevent the occupation from being rateable. Thus, a weekly tenant of a house has a sufficient degree of permanence for rateability, if occupation in fact continues for longer.

2.70 In the case of markets, rateability is not avoided because the market is only held on certain days. It is the occupier of the market as a whole, rather than individual stallholders, who would be rateable.

2.71 The character of the occupation is important as well as length. Short-term quarrying of nine months and even six months, because of the nature of the occupation, has been held sufficiently permanent, and a twelve-month working rule has been rejected.

Checklist

2.72 Liability to pay rates is an occupiers' liability. No occupier – no rates. Occupation includes actual possession (fact) and does not mean legal possession (title). If owners use land, they are rateable unless someone else occupies it. Four elements of rateable occupation exist.

2.73 Actual possession—unused property is not rateable. An intention to occupy is insufficient by itself. The use of land must result from positive acts. A slight user is sufficient.

2.74 Exclusive occupation—ie the ability to exclude everyone else from using the land in the same way. Where two occupiers use land in a similar way, it is the person who is in paramount control of the use made by others of the premises who has exclusive occupation. An owner in occupation is presumed to be the rateable occupier. Occupation must be exclusive in fact, not title. Paramount occupation is determined by control over the use of parts let.

2.75 Beneficial occupation—ie of value, not profitable. Will the occupation produce a rent? Land 'struck with sterility' is not capable of beneficial occupation.

2.76 Permanent occupation—this depends on duration of actual occupation (not on length of grant) and also on nature of occupation.

2.77 For rateable occupation to exist, all four elements must be present. The absence of any one of these will prevent rateability.

Chapter 3

Rateable property

Synopsis

3.1 'The occupier, not the land, is rateable; but the occupier is rateable in respect of the land which he occupies.' (*Westminster City Council v Southern Rail Co Ltd* (1936).)

3.2 Property on which an occupier is liable to pay rates is listed as land, houses, mines, sporting and advertising rights. All these are rateable property, unless excluded by statute.

3.3 Items of plant and machinery will only be rateable if listed by statute, and other chattels are rateable if they are occupied with and enhance the value of land.

3.4 The unit of rateable property which is actually assessed is the hereditament (see Chapter 4).

Property liable to rates

3.5 Property which is liable to be rated is listed (s 16) as *lands*, *houses*, coal mines, *mines* of any other description, and *sporting rights*. Section 28 gives details of the rating of *advertising rights*.

3.6 The word *'lands'* is taken to mean everything on or over, as well as the surface of, the land, and will, therefore, include *buildings* and areas of surface water.

3.7 Although it is often said that a particular property is rateable, this is not strictly true. It is the *occupier* who is rateable in respect of his occupation of property.

3.8 All land and buildings will be rateable property unless specifically exempted by statute (see Chapter 5).

3.9 *Chattels* are not normally rateable property, but they may be rated if they are occupied with and enhance the value of land. Thus, *caravans* and *builders' huts* are chattels, but once they are occupied with land and enhance its value, they will combine with the land to produce a rateable unit (*LCC* v *Wilkins (VO)* (1957)).

3.10   Under s 21, *chattels* which are *plant and machinery* are rateable property if the item of plant and machinery is specified in statute. It is then deemed to be part of the hereditament, which is assessed at its enhanced value. The value of any plant and machinery not listed is ignored in valuing the property (see 3.15–33).

3.11   Certain *incorporeal rights*, such as *easements*, *tolls* and *rights of common*, are rateable property if the exercise and enjoyment of them involves the exclusive occupation of land. It is the fact of occupation which will decide rateability, not the form of the legal title from which it is enjoyed (see Chapter 2).

3.12   Land used for a plantation or wood or for the growth of saleable underwood, and not subject to any right in common, which is occupied together with a house as a park, or is preserved mainly or exclusively for purposes of sport or recreation, is the only rateable *woodland*. Most woodland is exempt from rates as agricultural land (see Chapter 5).

3.13   *Advertising rights* are rateable as a separate hereditament generally where the right is occupied by someone other than the occupier of the land on which the right exists (see 3.46–60).

3.14   Although *mines*, both coal mines and 'mines of any other description', are rateable property, special provisions exist for valuing them (see Chapter 9).

Plant and machinery

(*Section 21 and Sched 3 of the 1967 Act, Plant and Machinery (Rating) Order 1960, Plant and Machinery (Rating) (Amendment) Order 1974.*)

3.15   An occupier is rateable in respect of all land unless statute provides otherwise, **but all plant and machinery is exempt unless it is specifically mentioned in statute**.

3.16   'Plant and machinery' is not *defined* but 'plant' was described as including 'whatever apparatus or instruments are used by a businessman in carrying on his business. The term does not include stock-in-trade, nor does it include the place in which the business is carried on' (*J Lyons & Co Ltd* v *A-G* (1944) quoting from *Yarmouth* v *France* (1887), a case involving industrial injury).

3.17   Rateable plant and machinery may or may not be an integral part of the hereditament. It may be *part of a hereditament* and thus increase the value of the hereditament, or it may form a *separate hereditament* and be valued as such.

3.18 However, only items of plant and machinery which are *mentioned in statute* will be treated this way. All other items must be ignored for rating purposes, unless the *profits method* of valuation is being used, in which case all items of plant and machinery must be included (s 21(1)) (see Chapter 9).

3.19 Generally, items are given their trade or technical names, the meaning of which can be explained by an expert witness. However, it was held in *Chesterfield Tube Co Ltd* v *Thomas (VO)* (1970) that:

> The question . . . is what they mean to rating valuers and surveyors, the occupiers of hereditaments and the practical technicians concerned with the design, making and operation of the plant and machinery which the hereditaments contain.

3.20 In *Union Cold Storage Co Ltd* v *Phillips (VO)* (1975) it was accepted that 'cold storage rooms' were 'chambers of refrigeration' and, as such, listed and rateable.

3.21 Schedule 3 of the 1967 Act (as amended by the Plant and Machinery (Rating) Order 1960 and the Plant and Machinery (Rating) (Amendment) Order 1974) sets out 'classes of machinery and plant deemed to be part of the hereditament' and, as such, rateable.

3.22 *Class 1A* lists plant and machinery (together with any accessories) 'which is or is intended to be used mainly or exclusively in connection with . . . the *generation, storage, primary transformation or main transmission of power* in or on the hereditament'.

Table 1A lists such accessories as steam boilers, furnaces, gas turbines, internal combustion engines, motor generators, switchboards, distribution boards, control panels and all switch gear, water wheels, and water turbines.

3.23 *Class 1B* lists plant and machinery (together with any accessories) 'which is used or intended to be used mainly or exclusively in connection with . . . the *heating, cooling, ventilating, lighting, draining or supplying of water to the land or buildings* . . . or the *protection of the hereditament from fire* . . .', provided that any of these items '. . . which is in or on the hereditament for the purpose of *manufacturing operations* or trade processes . . .' shall be considered as not listed (and, therefore, not rateable).

Table 1B includes water and gas heaters, refrigerating machines, plant for filtering and cooling, plug sockets and other outlets, sewage treatment plant and machinery, plant and machinery for the treatment of water, sprinkler and fire alarm systems. There is also a list of accessories which includes pipes, ducts, cables, supports and recording instruments.

3.24 *Class 2* specifies passenger *lifts* and elevators.

3.25 *Class 3* specifies railway and tramway *lines and tracks*.

3.26 *Class 4* lists a number of items under two tables, *Tables A* and *B*. Any of the listed items must be or be in the nature of a *building* or *structure* to be rateable, including any parts of the items which form an integral part.

However, any item or part 'which is moved or rotated by motive power as part of the process of manufacture' is excepted and, therefore, not rateable. Also excepted is 'any refractory or other lining forming part of any plant or machinery as is customarily renewed by reason of normal use at intervals of less than fifty weeks' (1974 amendment).

These conditions will affect items listed in *Table A* which include: *blast furnaces*, coking ovens, floating docks and pontoons, mine, quarry and pit headgear, television masts, slipways, loading and unloading platforms and stages, weighbridges and *windmills*.

3.27 In addition to the conditions mentioned above, the items listed under *Table B* will only be considered as listed (and, therefore, rateable) if the item has a total cubic capacity which exceeds 200 cubic metres and can readily be moved from one site and re-erected in its original state on another site without the substantial demolition either of the item or its surrounding structure.

Items listed in Table B include: accelerators, chambers for cooling, drying, refrigeration and testing, heat exchangers, reactors, *silos*, stills, *tanks*, cooling towers, water towers, *vats*, washeries and dry cleaners of coal, and wind tunnels.

3.28 *Class 5* specifies 'a *pipe* or *system of pipes* for the conveyance of anything'. Specifically exempted from this description is a drain or sewer, a pipe or pipe system vested in the gas or electricity authorities, or which forms part of the equipment of and is wholly located within a factory, petroleum storage depot, mine, quarry or mineral field.

3.29 Having established which items of plant and machinery are listed, and therefore rateable, it is necessary to determine whether the item forms part of a hereditament or constitutes a separate hereditament (see Chapter 4).

3.30 If an item of plant and machinery forms a *separate hereditament*, a valuation following normal rules to produce a *net annual value* directly is necessary (see Chapter 7).

3.31 If, however, items of plant and machinery are rateable as *part of the hereditament*, one assessment for the whole hereditament should be found. The land, buildings and rateable plant and machinery are treated as one unit and a single value produced. A separate value for the land, one for the buildings, and another for the rateable plant and machinery is not practicable where, for example, a factory unit comprises rateable plant and machinery for heating, lighting, drainage and supplying water. The whole property is valued in its entirety (see also 10.132–8).

3.32 There may, however, in any given case be good reasons for valuing separately such items of plant and machinery as central heating. For example, in using rents from comparable properties which do not have central heating, it will be necessary to add for central heating in the valuation of a factory which does have it.

3.33 This should highlight the need to appreciate what items of plant and machinery are involved in the assessment of any hereditament, especially since under s 21(2) the valuation officer can be required to give to the occupier written particulars of what plant and machinery has been deemed to be part of the hereditament and, therefore, included in the valuation.

Sporting rights (s 29)

3.34 Sporting rights are *incorporeal rights* which can either be assessed as *part of a hereditament* (in which case they increase the value of the land over which they are exercised), or they can form a *separate hereditament*.

3.35 Sporting rights which can be separately assessed are defined in s 16(*e*) as: 'any right of fowling, of shooting, of taking or killing game or rabbits or of fishing'.

3.36 When sporting rights are occupied together with the land over which the rights are exercised, the occupier of the land is rateable for the full value of the land including any value attributable to the sporting rights.

3.37 If the land is *agricultural land* (and therefore exempt from rates), the sporting rights are not rateable either.

3.38 Sporting rights will be separately assessed when they are severed from the occupation of the land over which they are enjoyed.

3.39 Where sporting rights are exercisable on non-agricultural land

and the right is in fact severed from the occupation of the land but is not let (ie the owner reserves the sporting rights) and the occupier pays rent for the land to the owner, then under s 29(1) the sporting right is not treated as a separate hereditament. The land is assessed at a value enhanced by the right and the occupier pays rates accordingly. However, the occupier may deduct the rates paid for the sporting rights from the rent.

3.40 Where any sporting right which is severed from the occupation of the land over which it is exercised is let, either the owner or lessee can be rated as the occupier of the right, at the discretion of the rating authority (s 29(2)).

3.41 *Severance* must normally be effected by deed for the purposes of s 29(2), but for s 29(1) a factual severance is sufficient.

3.42 Subject to the above provisions, the owner of any sporting rights which are severed from the occupation of land may be rated as the occupier (s 29(3)). Under this provision, if sporting rights are severed from the occupation of agricultural land, the owner can be rated in respect of them.

3.43 For the purposes of sporting rights, *owner* is defined in s 29(4) as '. . . the person who, if the right of sporting is not let, is entitled to exercise the right, or who, if the right is let, is entitled to receive the rent therefrom . . .'.

3.44 Where a sporting right forms a separate hereditament as a result of s 29, a *net annual value* is found directly.

3.45 Considerations which would affect the assessment have been held in *Myddleton* v *Charles (VO)* (1957) to be:

(a) the general nature of the country;
(b) the condition of coverts and woodlands;
(c) the extent of disturbing influences, such as roads, public footpaths and the proximity of unpreserved sporting rights; and
(d) the facilities for proper keepering and the degree of vermin infestation which, while not permanent, is likely to affect the head of game for a season or two.

Advertising rights (s 28)

3.46 Advertising rights are *incorporeal rights* which can either be assessed as *part of a hereditament* (in which case they increase the value of the land and buildings over which they are exercised) or they can form a *separate hereditament*.

3.47 An advertising right will be assessed as a separate hereditament where the right to use any land, wall or other part of a building, or any structure erected on the land, for advertising purposes, is let out or reserved to someone other than the occupier of the land.

3.48 It will also be assessed as a separate hereditament where the land is not used except for advertising purposes, and someone other than the owner exercises the advertising right (s 28(1)).

3.49 Because the right to advertise is *incorporeal*, its occupation is of necessity notional, ie it is not physically in possession, it is only notionally so in the right to receive rents.

3.50 Although the right to advertise is incorporeal, its value for rating purposes will include an appropriate amount for any structure etc made available for advertising purposes by the occupier of the land.

3.51 The separate hereditament will be treated as being created at the earlier of either the date when any sign or structure is erected after the right has been let out or reserved, or when any advertisement is exhibited under that right (s 28(2)).

3.52 When an advertising right constitutes a separate hereditament, provision exists (s 28(1)(*b*)) to prevent the value of that right increasing the value of the remaining land and buildings, thus avoiding assessing the advertising right twice.

3.53 The grant of an incorporeal right, such as an advertising right, is only valid when made by deed; however, since rating is not concerned with legal title, it seems that for rating purposes the right must be 'so let out as to be capable of separate assessment' (*Westminster City Council* v *Southern Rail Co Ltd* (1936)).

3.54 Where an advertising right is assessed as a separate hereditament, it will be valued directly to *net annual value* (see Chapter 7).

3.55 Where an advertising right is *assessed as part of a larger hereditament*, the enjoyment of the right is likely to enhance the value of the land and buildings, which should therefore be assessed at their enhanced value (s 28(4)).

3.56 Only where land and buildings are solely used to display advertisements, and that right is not let out or reserved to someone other than the occupier, will the person permitting the land to be used in this way be rateable. If that person cannot be found, the owner will be rateable (s 28(3)).

3.57 In this context, *owner* is defined (s 115) as

> . . . any person . . . receiving or entitled to receive the rack rent of the lands or premises . . . whether on his own account or as

agent or trustee for any other person, or who would so receive or be entitled to receive that rent if the lands or premises were let on a rack rent . . .

3.58 The provisions regarding the rating of advertising rights as a separate hereditament (s 28(1)) do not apply to the right to use any land which forms part of *railway or canal premises*, which are *used for non-rateable purposes*, for the display of advertisements. Thus, advertising rights on non-rateable railway or canal premises cannot form separate (ie rateable) hereditaments.

3.59 'Railway or canal premises' are defined in s 32(1) as premises which are occupied by the British Railways Board, the London Transport Board and the British Waterways Board. 'Non-rateable purposes' involve all purposes of these boards' undertakings '. . . which are concerned with the carriage of goods or passengers by rail or inland waterway or the provision of the facilities for traffic by inland waterway . . .' together with all 'subsidiary or incidental purposes' to the above.

3.60 Under s 32(7)(*c*), where railway or canal premises are occupied by one of these boards partly for non-rateable purposes and partly for the display of advertisements, the display of advertisements is deemed to be a non-rateable purpose.

Checklist

3.61 Property on which rates may be levied comprises all land and buildings (including houses), all mines and, when assessed as separate hereditaments, sporting rights and advertising rights.

3.62 Land and buildings are rateable unless specifically exempted.

3.63 Chattels are exempt, but may be rateable together with land if they are occupied with and enhance the value of the land.

3.64 Items of plant and machinery are exempt unless they are specifically listed in statute.

3.65 Incorporeal hereditaments are rateable if the occupier is in exclusive occupation.

3.66 Sporting and advertising rights may increase the value of the land with which they are assessed or they may form separate rateable units.

3.67 In order to be assessed to rates, rateable property must form a rateable unit, ie a hereditament.

Chapter 4

The hereditament

Synopsis

4.1 Property on which an occupier is liable to pay rates is listed as lands, houses, mines, sporting and advertising rights. All these are rateable property unless excluded by statute.

4.2 Generally, the rateable property on which rates are actually levied is the unit of occupation; legal ownership is not normally relevant for rate liability.

4.3 The unit of rateable property which is actually assessed is the hereditament. A hereditament is a separate entry in the valuation list and each has a rateable value.

4.4 A hereditament must not only be rateable property but must also conform to certain criteria. It must be: capable of definition; a single geographical entity; capable of separate occupation; put to a single use; and exist within a single rating area.

Definition

4.5 The unit of rateable property which may be assessed for rating purposes is a *hereditament*. Statute gives little guidance as to what a hereditament is, although s 115 states that a '*hereditament* means property which is or may become liable to a rate, being a unit of such property which is, or would fall to be, shown as a separate item in the valuation list'.

4.6 The *valuation list* is, basically, a volume containing entries of every unit of rateable property on which rates may be levied in any rating area, together with the values on which rates are based (see Chapter 11 Appendix 4, item 7). To define a 'hereditament' as being a unit of rateable property which is a separate entry in the valuation list presup-

26

poses knowledge of what a hereditament is before it can be entered into the valuation list.

4.7 In other words, if rateable property is to be a hereditament, it must be a separate entry in the valuation list; but it cannot be a separate entry until it is a hereditament.

4.8 Fortunately, it is possible to refer to case law which extends this definition so that a hereditament must:

(a) be capable of physical definition;
(b) be a single geographical unit;
(c) be capable of separate occupation;
(d) be put to a single use;
(e) exist within a single rating area.

4.9 Rateable property must conform to each of these criteria if it is to be a hereditament and, therefore, liable to be rated. Each of these criteria will be considered in detail.

A hereditament must be capable of physical definition

4.10 It must always be possible to identify the actual land (or other rateable property) which is to be assessed, even if no physical boundaries exist.

4.11 Where a golf club had a licence to use an undefined area of the New Forest for a golf course, it was held that no hereditament was defined, so that there was nothing in respect of which the club could be assessed for rates (*Peak (VO)* v *Burley Golf Club* (1960)).

4.12 A market stall was held to be not rateable, because no right was given for it to be fixed on any definite portion of ground (*Spear* v *Bodmin Union* (1880)). (Had the land on which the stall stood been capable of definition, the land, together with the stall (which was a chattel), would have combined to form rateable property and a hereditament capable of assessment.)

A hereditament must be a single geographical unit

4.13 A hereditament must form a single geographical unit, so that two properties which are *divided by property in the occupation of another* will always be two separate hereditaments (provided, of course, that they conform to the other criteria) (*Gilbert (VO)* v *Hickinbottom & Sons Ltd* (1956)).

4.14 Where two properties in the same occupation are contiguous (and conform to the other criteria), they may be one hereditament.

4.15 *Contiguous*, in this context, means 'touching', not 'adjacent' or 'close'. Premises on the opposite sides of a road will be contiguous if the highway is in the exclusive occupation of the occupier of the premises (but see *Gilbert (VO)* v *Hickinbottom & Sons Ltd* (1956)). Connections by cables, pipes, wires or railway lines will not create contiguity.

4.16 In one case, a university occupied a number of buildings in the town beyond the main campus. Although functionally part of the university, the buildings were scattered throughout the town and, there-fore, the university's occupation of the campus and the individual properties was split by properties in the occupation of others. Each separate property formed a separate hereditament, all in the occupation of the university (*Glasgow University* v *Glasgow Assessor* (1952)—although a Scottish case and not binding on English law, it is considered to be persuasive).

4.17 Similarly, occupiers of flats with garages may find that the flat and garage are two separate hereditaments since, although they are both in the same occupation, they are not contiguous (ie touching) and because they are physically separated by property in the occupation of (an)other(s).

4.18 This should also apply to suites of offices within a single office building. However, in *British Railways Board* v *Hopkins (VO) and Birmingham District Council* (1981) the Board occupied the lower ground, ground and first floors, together with the fifth to tenth floors inclusive of a purpose-built office block. The remaining floors were vacant and available for letting. The case revolved (in part) on whether the parts occupied constituted a single hereditament or whether the whole building should be a single hereditament.

In deciding that the normal rules should apply to the identification of a hereditament (the fact that there were special statutory procedures for the valuation of railway premises being irrelevant) the Lands Tribunal stated:

> No-one suggests in the present case that the fifth to tenth floors should be separately assessed from the lower ground, ground and first floors on the grounds that they are not contiguous. With that possible qualification the occupied premises satisfy the definition of the hereditament . . .

4.19 A *functional connection* between two non-contiguous properties may cause them to be treated as a single hereditament (see 4.29).

A hereditament must be capable of separate occupation

4.20 Where one property is capable of being separately occupied, for example a single dwellinghouse occupied by a single family unit, that is a single hereditament.

4.21 Where one property is capable of being occupied by several occupiers, for example a single block of six self-contained flat units, each flat is a separate hereditament and the whole block comprises six hereditaments.

4.22 Where several properties which are contiguous are *in the same occupation*, they will be treated as forming a single hereditament unless, for some *special reason*, they must be treated as separate hereditaments, such as where properties are situated in different rating areas or where one property is used for a different purpose (*Gilbert (VO)* v *Hickinbottom & Sons Ltd* (1956)).

4.23 Thus, shop units in a purpose-built block may be contiguous and, even without being internally connected, may be a single hereditament if they are occupied by the same occupier and used for a single (or several related) purpose(s).

4.24 In considering whether a property is capable of separate occupation, any *structural alterations* which would be necessary for separate occupation must be ignored.

4.25 However, a single property may, in fact, be occupied by several occupiers, and thereby comprise several hereditaments, even though the occupations are not structurally divided, eg several tenants sharing a physically unaltered house.

A hereditament must be put to a single use

4.26 Several properties which are contiguous and in the same occupation will be a single hereditament if they are used for a single purpose, regardless of whether each is capable of separate occupation.

4.27 Where *living accommodation* adjoins and is occupied and used in connection with *business premises*, it will normally be considered as being used for the same purpose as the business premises, and thus form a single hereditament with the business premises (*Heath* v *Mitcalfe (VO)* (1957)).

4.28 Premises which may form a single hereditament if in the same occupation must be 'contiguous' If premises are in one occupation but are physically separated by property in the occupation of another, they cannot be a single hereditament, regardless of their use (see 4.15–16).

4.29 However, if premises in one occupation are physically separated by property which is not occupied by anyone else, there may be a single hereditament if there is a strong enough *functional dependency* between them.

4.30 Where premises are used together, but each is situated either side of a public highway, then if they are so essential in use the one to another, they should be regarded as one hereditament (*Gilbert (VO)* v *Hickinbottom & Sons Ltd* (1956)).

4.31 If several buildings in one occupation are physically separated, being interspersed among buildings in other occupations, they cannot be a single hereditament. It is only because the road is not in the rateable occupation of anyone that the functional test can be applied.

4.32 The cases in which the Lands Tribunal has applied the functional test to overcome geographical separation of premises appear to fall into two categories:

  (a) where a manufacturing process is carried on in both premises; or
  (b) where a manufacturing process is carried on in one property and what goes on in the other is essential to prevent a breakdown.

4.33 The Lands Tribunal has referred to the analogy of a sparking plug (*Edwards (VO)* v *BP Refinery (Llandarcy) Ltd* (1974)):

> . . . where the gap between the two parts is so small that it can physically be traversed in the course of the functioning of the whole . . . the stronger the spark the greater the gap which can be traversed.

A hereditament must exist within one rating area

4.34 Rates are levied on property within each rating area (all hereditaments are entered into the valuation list, one valuation list being prepared for each rating area).

4.35 If property would otherwise comprise a single hereditament but happens to be divided by a local authority boundary, *two artificial hereditaments* must be created so that two rating assessments can be entered, one into each valuation list for the two rating areas.

4.36 The other normal rules for ascertaining a hereditament will be observed in order to produce the appropriate value. Once values have been established, two artificial hereditaments are created, so that one entry into each valuation list can be made, and the single valuation is split between the two artificial hereditaments.

Hereditaments created by statute

4.37 The above criteria, as defined by case law, extend the statutory definition of 'hereditament'. However, statute has laid down certain circumstances in which property which would normally comprise several hereditaments may be treated as a single hereditament, in the occupation of the owner (see Chapter 6).

House adapted for occupation in parts

(See also 6.27–35.)

4.38 Where a purpose-built *dwellinghouse* (or a building structurally adapted as a purpose-built dwellinghouse) is, in fact, *occupied in parts* by several rateable occupiers, the valuation officer, in assessing the property, may decide that rather than value each separate occupation as a separate hereditament (under the normal rules), he will exercise his *discretion* under s 24 and assess the whole property as a *single hereditament*.

4.39 Should he decide to assess the whole property as a single hereditament, the rateable occupier will be deemed to be '. . . the person who receives the rents payable in respect of the parts', ie *the owner*.

4.40 In exercising his discretion, the valuation officer must have 'regard to *all the circumstances of the case*, including the extent, if any, to which the parts separately occupied have been severed by *structural alterations*' and, provided he has done so, the court cannot substitute its own discretion in place of that of the valuation officer (*Lewis-Jones* v *Williams (VO) and Cardiff City Council* (1970)). All the court can do is ensure that the valuation officer has had 'regard to all the circumstances'. (The right to challenge the assessment of a hereditament which has been treated in this way exists under s 69(1)—see Chapters 6 and 12).

4.41 The reason for the introduction of the s 24 provisions appears to be purely to facilitate the rating authority's rate collection.

4.42 It seems that rate collection in dwellinghouses which are let to several occupiers causes rating authorities problems in certain cases, and that making an owner liable for the payment of rates gives not only a fixed source of rate payment but also more certainty of rate receipt.

4.43 The owner will collect rates together with rent from the occupiers of the various parts of the dwelling on a more frequent basis than the rating authority could have done, and any problems the rating authority may have had with transient occupiers not paying rates are minimised.

Leisure caravan sites

(*Rating (Caravan Sites) Act 1976*—see also 10.215–18.)

4.44 Where a chattel (such as a caravan) is placed on a piece of land and is occupied with and enhances the value of that land, it will combine with that land to form one unit of occupation (*Field Place Caravan Park Ltd* v *Harding (VO)* (1966)). Thus, provided the caravan remains standing for a sufficient length of time (at least a year, it seems) it will become a rateable hereditament together with the land on which it stands.

4.45 The Rating (Caravan Sites) Act 1976 amends the provisions for separately rating caravans by giving the valuation officer discretion to assess leisure caravan sites as a *single hereditament in the occupation of the site operator*.

4.46 The discretion relates only to leisure caravan sites, not residential caravan sites, and can be exercised if:

(a) the leisure caravan site exceeds 334.45 square metres (400 square yards);

(b) the individual leisure caravans are or would be separate hereditaments but for the Rating (Caravan Sites) Act 1976;

(c) there is a restriction preventing the site from being occupied all the year round (ie excluding residential caravan sites from these provisions).

4.47 Should the valuation officer choose to exercise his discretion, the individual pitches plus any other areas of the site, eg toilet blocks, will all be assessed as one hereditament *in the occupation of the site operator*.

4.48 Provisions exist to ensure that a caravan occupier would not pay less rates if the caravans were treated as a single hereditament than if the whole site was treated as a single hereditament (Rating (Caravan Sites) Act 1976, s 1(7)).

4.49 Provision is also made to ensure the display by the site operator of a statement by the valuation officer of how many caravans are included in the single hereditament and the aggregate of rateable values attributable to them (Rating (Caravan Sites) Act 1976, s 2).

4.50   The Rating (Caravan Sites) Act 1976 thus *facilitates rate collection*. The rating authority no longer has to deal with occupiers who are only resident for part of the year. Rates can be collected from the site operator who passes on the burden to the caravan occupiers and collect rates together with rent (see Chapter 6).

Occupation of a hereditament where only part is used

4.51   In the case of a dwellinghouse, if the occupier makes use of only some of the rooms, he is still rateable for the whole (*R* v *Aberystwith* (1808)).

4.52   Generally, if a hereditament is only partly used, rateability can only be avoided by giving up occupation of the whole property. (*Occupation of part is occupation of whole*.)

4.53   Under s 25(2) the rating authority has a *discretionary power* in certain cases to reduce the rates paid on a hereditament which is partly unoccupied. Provided the hereditament is going to remain *unoccupied for a short time only*, '. . . the rating authority *may* request the valuation officer to *apportion the rateable value* of the hereditament between the occupied and unoccupied parts . . .'.

4.54   The apportionment must be agreed between the valuation officer and the rating authority. The apportioned value will be treated as the rateable value, and rates paid on that apportioned value until the unoccupied part is reoccupied.

4.55   There is no provision for the occupier to claim or enforce a reduction if either the rating authority refuses to request an apportionment from the valuation officer, or the rating authority and the valuation officer cannot agree on the apportionment.

4.56   Section 25 does not apply to a hereditament for which the owner pays rates instead of the occupier (ss 55 and 56—see Chapter 6), but it does apply to one where the owner has agreed merely to collect rates on behalf of the rating authority (s 56—see Chapter 6).

Checklist

4.57   The statutory definition of 'hereditament' (s 115), ie rateable property which is a separate item in the valuation list, is extended by case law. Thus, a hereditament must:

(a) be capable of physical definition;
(b) be a single geographical unit, ie within the same curtilage or contiguous, and not divided by property in the occupation of another;
(c) be capable of separate occupation or be, in fact, in one occupation;
(d) be put to a single use: a functional connection may allow properties which are not contiguous to be a single hereditament provided they are not divided by property in the occupation of another;
(e) exist within one rating area: if not, two artificial hereditaments are created for each valuation list. The total valuation is unaffected, just apportioned.

4.58 Where hereditaments are created by statute:

(a) 'house adapted for occupation in parts' (s 24)—where a single dwelling is occupied in parts, the valuation officer has discretion (subject to certain conditions) to assess the whole dwelling as a single hereditament in the occupation of the owner;
(b) leisure caravan sites (Rating (Caravan Sites) Act 1976)—the valuation officer has discretion (subject to certain conditions) to assess the whole site as a single hereditament in the occupation of the site operator.

4.59 Where only part of a hereditament is used, s 25 gives the rating authority discretion (under certain circumstances) to request an apportionment of the rateable value and to levy rates on the apportioned value.

Chapter 5

Exemptions and reliefs

Synopsis

5.1 Occupiers are rateable in respect of their occupation of all land and buildings, unless statute states otherwise.

5.2 Total exemption from liability to rates can be achieved by either:

   (a) exempting the property from being liable to assessment, so that the occupier has no liability to pay rates; or

   (b) exempting the occupier from rates in respect of the property he occupies; or

   (c) giving a rating authority the power not to demand rates normally recoverable.

5.3 Partial exemption or relief from the full burden of rates can take the following forms:

   (a) by varying the normal rules of valuation or procedure for a particular class of hereditament, a lower rateable value can be achieved, thus reducing the rate liability;

   (b) by the provision of rate rebates, the rating authority can ease the rate burden on individual ratepayers;

   (c) by reducing the rate in the pound levied by rating authorities on any given class or classes of hereditament, a reduced rate liability can result;

   (d) by altering the relationship between net annual value and rateable value (derating—normally net annual value is the same as rateable value), a reduced rate liability can result;

   (e) by altering statutory deductions from a gross value which has been arrived at by normal valuation processes. This can alter the rateable value and, over a range of gross values, the relationship between higher and lower gross values can be affected.

35

5.4 All these methods of exemption and relief are, or have been, employed in reducing liability to rates. The current situation is set out in this chapter.

Exempted property

5.5 Occupiers are liable to rates in respect of all land and buildings unless specifically exempted.

5.6 The following land and buildings are specifically exempt from rates.

Agricultural land and buildings

5.7 Statutory provisions relating to agricultural land and buildings are contained in s 26 as amended by the Rating Act 1971, the Rating Enactments (Agricultural Land and Agricultural Buildings) (Amendment) Regulations 1978 and s 31 of the Local Government Planning and Land Act 1980.

5.8 No agricultural land or agricultural buildings shall be liable to be rated or included in any valuation list (s 26(1)).

(a) Agricultural land

5.9 'Agricultural land' is defined in the statutes mentioned in 5.7 to comprise any land used as: *arable*, *meadow* or *pasture ground*; woodland; land exceeding 0.1 hectare used for poultry farming or cottage gardens; market gardens; nursery grounds; orchards; allotments; land occupied together with an agricultural building (see 5.12) and land used solely for or in connection with fish farming.

5.10 To benefit from the exemption, land must be *solely used* for these purposes and additional uses, such as use of land as gallops by horse trainers (*Forster* v *Simpson (VO)* (1984)) will prevent the land qualifying for the exemption. However, the principle of *de minimis* is applied (ie a slight non-rateable use may be permitted) so that the use of agricultural land for a local agricultural show held on one day a year will not cause the land to be treated as rateable (*Honiton & District Agricultural Association* v *Wonnocott* (1955)).

5.11 The following are specifically *excluded from the definition* of agricultural land: land occupied together with a house as a park or gardens; pleasure grounds, land kept or preserved mainly or exclusively for sport or recreation; or land used as a racecourse. Thus, woodlands (which are usually exempt as agricultural land) will not fall within the definition of agricultural land if they are occupied together with a house as a park or garden.

(b) Agricultural buildings

5.12 'Agricultural buildings' include *buildings occupied together with agricultural land and used solely in connection with agricultural operations on that land* (s 26). An agricultural building may also be occupied by a farming syndicate provided that either the syndicate or all its individual members rateably occupy agricultural land (Rating Act 1971, s 26).

5.13 'Occupied together with' means a functional rather than geographical connection, and it is not therefore necessary to have an agricultural building situated on the agricultural land with which it is occupied. However, it must be possible to identify agricultural land together with which the buildings are solely used.

5.14 Any use of a building for non-agricultural purposes will exclude the building from the definition of agricultural buildings.

5.15 The above definition is extended (by the Rating Act 1971) to include the following buildings which are solely used for agricultural operations but which are not 'occupied together with' agricultural land:

(a) buildings used for the *keeping and breeding of livestock* and ancillary buildings;

(b) buildings occupied and used for *the keeping of bees*;

(c) certain buildings *occupied by a corporate body* and used in connection with agricultural operations on agricultural land.

5.16 The extension of the definition to include 'factory farms' and buildings used for keeping bees is limited by the requirement that the buildings be contiguous to or surrounded by at least two hectares of agricultural land. It is irrelevant who owns or occupies the agricultural land.

5.17 The definition of agricultural buildings is further extended to include buildings used solely for or in connection with *fish farming* (LGPLA 1980, s 31).

5.18 In no case is a dwellinghouse an agricultural building (s 25) (see 5.63 and 10.39 for agricultural dwellinghouses).

Parks and pleasure grounds (s 44)

5.19   As explained earlier, the public is not a legal entity and cannot, therefore, be a rateable occupier (see 2.56). In cases where the public has such extensive rights to use land that all value to an occupier is lost, that occupier is not in rateable occupation of that land. Thus, a highway is not in rateable occupation of the public or of the highway authority.

5.20   In addition to the normal rules for ascertaining whether there is a rateable occupier (see Chapter 2), s 44 states that a park provided by or under the management of a local authority, which is available for free and unrestricted use by the public, shall be treated as if it had been dedicated in perpetuity for such use.

5.21   This effectively renders the land 'struck with sterility' and, as such, not rateable (see 2.56).

5.22   Within s 44 'park' includes a recreation or pleasure ground, public walk, open space and a playing field.

Churches and church halls etc

5.23   Churches, although not specifically exempt from rates until 1833, have never been rated in practice. The current statutory provisions (s 39) exempt from rates:

> (a) ***Places of public religious worship*** which belong to either the Church in England or the Church in Wales or which are certified as required by law as places of religious worship. Such places need not be exclusively used for public religious worship. The use for other purposes (eg meetings, recreational activities) will not prevent the exemption unless it renders the churches incapable of being used for public religious worship or unless it involves a letting for profit (see 5.26).
>
> (b) '***Any church hall***, chapel hall or similar building ***used in connection with any such place of public religious worship***, and so used for the purposes of the organisation responsible for the conduct of public religious worship in that place.'

5.24   Such halls or buildings are exempt whether they form a separate hereditament or part of a hereditament together with the place of public religious worship with which they are used. Again, there is no requirement as to exclusive use, but these buildings should be predominantly used as described.

5.25 What is essential, however, is that the building is 'used in connection with' a place of public religious worship (*Church House Trustees v Dimmick (VO) (1959)*).

5.26 Where a place of public religious worship or its church hall etc is *let at a profit*, the exemption from rates is lost for the next full rate period only, the gross value being the profit attributable to the letting.

Enterprise zones

5.27 Schedule 32, para 27 of the LGPLA 1980 exempts from liability to rates certain hereditaments during such time as the locality in which they are situated is designated an enterprise zone.

5.28 Entries, including values, are still to be made in the valuation list, but no rates are levied.

5.29 An *exempt hereditament* is one which is *not*:

    (a) a domestic hereditament, ie a dwellinghouse, private garage, or private storage premises (defined in 10.55–7);

    (b) a public utility hereditament, specified in Sched 3 to the Local Government Act 1974 (eg water, rail, gas etc);

    (c) a public utility hereditament valued on the profits basis.

5.30 *All other hereditaments within an enterprise zone are exempt from payment of rates.*

5.31 In the case of *mixed hereditaments* (ie a hereditament partly comprising residential use and partly comprising some other use—see 5.96 and 5.102–4) situated within an enterprise zone, the portion of rateable value attributable to the dwelling part is determined by the valuation officer, and rates will be levied on that rateable value as if the whole hereditament was a private dwelling.

Non-domestic hereditaments not in active use

5.32 Where a non-domestic hereditament is rateable only because *plant, machinery or equipment used or to be used in the hereditament is kept there*, under s 46A(1) of the 1967 Act (inserted by the Rates Act 1984) it is treated as unoccupied.

5.33 This treatment, together with the Rating (Exemption of Unoccupied Industrial and Storage Hereditaments) Regulations 1985 (which suspend the powers of the rating authorities to levy rates on unoccupied 'industrial and storage hereditaments'—see 6.47) effectively exempts from rates so-called *'mothballed' factories*.

5.34 Under s 46A, a non-domestic hereditament is defined as any hereditament which is not a dwellinghouse, private garage or private storage premises.

Miscellaneous exemptions of land and buildings

5.35 The occupation of the following properties is exempt from any liability to rates:

(a) *lighthouses*, *buoys* and *beacons* etc occupied by any general lighthouse authority (Merchant Shipping Act 1894, s 731, as amended by s 41);

(b) *sewers*, *manholes*, *pumping stations* etc (s 42);

(c) *land structures or appliances occupied or maintained by drainage authorities* (s 43);

(d) *air raid protection works* provided that they are used '. . . solely for the purpose of affording protection in the event of hostile attack from the air . . .' (s 46);

(e) *rooms used for elections* or holding public meetings for the furtherance of anyone's candidature, in premises not otherwise rateable, shall not render those properties liable to be rated (Sched 2, paras 18 and 22(1) of the Representation of the People Act 1949).

Exempted occupiers

5.36 As well as exempting property, *an occupier can be exempted* from liability to pay rates. In other words, the exemption depends on who the rateable occupier is, not on the type of property he occupies.

The Crown

5.37 Because of the general rule that the Crown is only bound by statutes which specifically relate to it, and because the Crown was not specifically mentioned in the Poor Relief Act 1601 (or any subsequent rating Act), the Crown is not statutorily liable to pay rates.

5.38 The exemption depends entirely on the fact that *the property is occupied by the Crown*, and not that the property is owned by the Crown. Lands in the ownership of the Crown will be rateable when someone other than the Crown is the occupier. (Rating liability does not depend on legal title, only actual possession—see 2.15.)

5.39 However, *occupation by servants* of the Crown will also be exempt if the nature of the servant's occupation is such that it is deemed to be occupation by the master.

5.40 The exemption is further extended to include cases where property is occupied for the *purposes of government*, which are considered to be the purposes of the Crown. Thus, occupation by departments of state, the military and admiralty, police, law courts and prisons are all government purposes and therefore exempt from rates under the Crown exemption.

5.41 It is, therefore, important to consider the *object of the occupation* as well as the occupier, to establish where the Crown is in fact or in effect the occupier and, therefore, exempt from rates.

5.42 Hereditaments used as local authority administrative offices are not exempt under these provisions. Generally, the various statutory corporations established to run the nationalised industries and other undertakings are not servants of the Crown for the purposes of an exemption from rates (*BBC* v *Johns* (1965); Iron and Steel Act 1982, s 13(1)).

5.43 However, any land occupied by the Atomic Energy Authority is deemed to be 'occupied by or on behalf of the Crown for public purposes' (Atomic Energy Act 1954, s 6(1)) and, therefore, exempt from any liability to pay rates.

5.44 Although no assessment is made for any hereditament exempt under these provisions, the Crown may make a voluntary *contribution* towards the rates in rating areas where certain exempt property exists.

5.45 The contribution is determined by a government valuer (the Treasury Valuer) and may be paid in respect of property occupied, for example, by the police and for the administration of justice. In such cases the value on which the contribution is based is entered into the valuation list as representing the rateable value of the hereditament. Such entries are often grouped together within the valuation list and called 'contribution cases'.

Foreign sovereigns and diplomats

5.46 Under common law, foreign sovereigns and diplomats are exempt from the process of the English courts. If a demand for rates were served, there would be no means of enforcing payment.

5.47 This effective exemption from rates is made statutory in the

Diplomatic Privileges Act 1964 which exempts the foreign state and the head of the mission from 'municipal dues and taxes' on property occupied for the purposes of their mission, including the residence of the head of the mission.

Relief granted by rating authorities

5.48   As well as exempting specific property and occupiers, from rates, statute has given rating authorities *power to waive their rights to collect rates* otherwise payable.

Charitable and similar organisations

5.49   There was a time when charities were considered not rateable because of their lack of beneficial occupation, but once it was established that profitability was not a requirement of beneficial occupation, charitable and similar organisations became rateable occupiers (see 2.52).

5.50   Under s 40 (see also Rating (Disabled Persons) Act 1978, s 2) two kinds of relief are available.

5.51   *Mandatory relief* of half the rates payable is granted to any hereditament *occupied by a charity* and used wholly or mainly for charitable purposes, and to an almshouse (s 40(1)).

5.52   Registration under the Charities Act 1960 is conclusive proof that an organisation is a charity for these purposes. (However, certain charities listed in Sched 8 are excluded from these provisions, eg the Universities of Bristol, London, Reading and Wales and the colleges and halls in the Universities of Oxford and Cambridge.)

5.53   The exemption will cover houses provided for the staff of a charity under the rule that occupation by a servant is occupation by his master (*Hirst* v *Sargent* (1966)).

5.54   It is a further requirement of s 40 that the hereditament should be *'wholly or mainly used for charitable purposes'*. A shop selling goods manufactured by the blind is entitled to relief under these provisions since the sale of goods directly facilitates the charitable object of providing employment for the blind. Under the Rating (Charity Shops) Act 1976, a hereditament shall be treated as wholly or mainly used for charitable purposes if used for the sale of goods donated to a charity, and all the net proceeds of sale are applied for the purposes of that charity.

5.55   Relief under s 40(1)(*a*) must be claimed in writing from the rating authority, and the amount of relief given cannot exceed one-half the amount of rates otherwise chargeable.

5.56 *Discretionary relief* of only half or all the rates due is available under s 40(5) to:

(a) any hereditament entitled to mandatory relief, ie occupied by a *charity* or an *almshouse*;

(b) any hereditament occupied by a *non-profit-making institution or organisation* the main objects of which are *charitable* or *otherwise* philanthropic, religious, educational, or concerned with social welfare, science, literature or the fine arts; and

(c) any other hereditament occupied by a *club*, society or other organisation not established or conducted for profit and which is wholly or mainly *used for recreation*.

5.57 In cases (b) and (c) the occupation must be for the charitable or other purposes of the organisation.

5.58 The relief is granted (and can be removed) at the discretion of the rating authority.

5.59 Relief available under s 40, whether mandatory or discretionary, is not available to places of public religious worship and ancillary buildings, which are exempt from rates under s 39 (see 5.23–6).

Poverty

5.60 Rates were originally introduced as a tax to provide funds to relieve the suffering of the poor. It is therefore illogical to expect the poor to contribute.

5.61 Under s 53, the rating authorities have the power to reduce or remit the payment of rates on the grounds of the poverty of the ratepayer, and under s 15 of the Local Government Act 1974 the rating authority may reduce or remit the payment of rates by an owner on the grounds of the poverty of the owner (see also Chapter 6).

Variation of the normal rules or procedure

5.62 Relief from rate liability may be achieved by varying the normal rules of valuation or procedure which are to apply in the case of any particular class of property. This is currently applied to two classes of hereditament.

Agricultural dwellinghouses

5.63 An agricultural dwellinghouse (see also 10.39–44) is not an 'agricultural building' and is not, therefore, exempt from rates (s 26(4)).

5.64 An *agricultural dwellinghouse* is *defined as* a house occupied in connection with agricultural land and used as the dwelling of a person who is primarily engaged in carrying on or directing agricultural or fish farming operations on that land or is employed in agricultural operations on that land in the service of the occupier of that land and is entitled to occupy the house only while so employed (s 26 as amended by LGPLA 1980, s 31).

5.65 The usual method of valuation for a dwellinghouse is to assess a gross value (s 19(6)—see 7.11), ie:

> the rent at which the hereditament might reasonably be expected to let from year to year if the tenant undertook to pay all usual tenant's rates and taxes and the landlord undertook to bear the cost of the repairs and insurance and the other expenses, if any, necessary to maintain the hereditament in a state to command that rent.

5.66 However, for as long as the house is occupied in connection with agricultural land and used as the dwelling of a person primarily engaged in or employed in agricultural operations on that land (see 5.64) then it is classed as an agricultural dwellinghouse and its *gross value* is 'estimated by reference to the rent at which the house might reasonably be expected to let from year to year if it could not be occupied and used other than as aforesaid' (s 26(2)).

5.67 The effect of this is to limit the rental bids which can be considered for the agricultural dwellinghouse to those payable by actual or potential occupiers engaged or employed in agricultural operations on agricultural land. This may depress the rent and thus the gross value and the rateable value (which is based on the gross value) and ultimately the rates paid. This reduction in rental value should be proven by rental evidence in the open market—see Chapter 9.

Dwellinghouses (minor structural alterations)

5.68 Because many people felt that when they improved their properties they were penalised with increased rates, s 21(1) of the Local Government Act 1974 allowed some measure of relief when minor structural alterations are made to dwellings (see also 10.23–38).

5.69 Under the normal rules of rating, once structural alterations are carried out on a hereditament, the valuation officer, who has a duty to ensure that the valuation list is correct, should alter the valuation list to take into account the structural alterations (assuming that they alter the rental value and, therefore, the rateable value and/or description of the hereditament). This is done by the use of a 'Proposal to alter the valuation list' as a result of which the appropriate entry in the list can be altered to take into account the structural alterations (see Chapters 7 and 12).

5.70 However, where only *minor structural alterations* (as defined) are made to a dwellinghouse, or *central heating* is installed in an occupied dwelling, s 21(1) of the Local Government Act 1974 *prevents* anyone making a *proposal to increase the assessment* of that hereditament to take into account the structural alterations or central heating.

5.71 Under s 21(1)(*a*) of the Local Government Act 1974, in respect of a dwellinghouse or mixed hereditament (ie a hereditament comprising partly residential accommodation and partly any other use— see 5.96), '*no proposal may be made* . . . for an increase in the gross value . . . by reason of *the making of structural alterations on or after 1 April 1974* . . . if the proposal would be for an increase *not exceeding* . . .' *£30*.

5.72 *Minor structural alterations* are thus defined within the Act (and the Rating of Minor Structural Alterations to Dwellings (Specified Amount) Order 1974) as including *alterations which do not increase the gross value of the hereditament by more than £30*. It is, therefore, a matter of valuation in any individual case as to what constitutes a minor structural alteration. It seems likely that a small kitchen extension or garage will be covered by this section.

5.73 Also under s 21(1)(*b*) of the Local Government Act 1974, in respect of a dwellinghouse or mixed hereditament:

> *no proposal may be made* . . . for an increase in the gross value . . . by reason of the making of structural alterations on or after 1 April 1974 . . . if . . . *the alterations are necessary for the purpose of installing a system for providing heating* in two or more rooms in the hereditament.

5.74 There is no value limit on the installation of central heating, so that any system installed after 1 April 1974 will not increase the gross value of the hereditament. However, additions to an existing heating system are not covered by this section and will therefore be taken into account in the gross value as normal (*Re Maudsley (VO) (1984)*).

5.75 Section 21 does not permit a valuer to ignore the effects of minor structural alterations or central heating but, having carried out a normal valuation of the dwelling, s 21 prevents a proposal being made to increase the gross value by more than £30 because of the minor structural alteration, or by any amount because of the addition of central heating. (There is no value limit on central heating.)

5.76 Thus, for example, if a garage is added to a dwellinghouse in 1980 and the increase in gross value is £20, no proposal may be made to increase the gross value as it would be for an amount not exceeding £30—precluded by s 21(1)(*a*) of the Local Government Act 1974. If, however, in 1984 a kitchen extension is added to the same dwellinghouse, which increases its gross value by £25, the overall increase in gross value which is not reflected in the valuation list will be £45 (£20 + £25), and a proposal *can* be made to increase an assessment by more than £30.

5.77 However, by limiting the relief to a procedural inability to increase the entry shown in the valuation list, as opposed to ignoring the increase in value altogether, the use of s 21(1) Local Government Act 1974 gave rise to *Dalby (VO)* v *Griffiths* (1976) and *Dalby (VO)* v *Lever* (1976) in which a reduction in gross value for a nuisance was claimed following the addition of central heating and an extension, covered by ss 21(1)(*a*) and (*b*) respectively.

5.78 In *Dalby (VO)* v *Griffiths* the court held that the provisions of s 21 did not affect the valuation of the hereditament, and that additions for central heating and structural alterations must be taken into account together with deductions for nuisances. Having arrived at a correct valuation, s 21 should be considered and the question asked: Will the proposal to give effect to the correct valuation increase the gross value by an amount exceeding £30? If the answer is no, the proposal is precluded by s 21 Local Government Act 1974, and the existing entry in the valuation list remains unaltered.

5.79 If the net result is a decrease in the existing gross value, a proposal can be made to give effect to that decrease and s 21 has no effect in that case (for valuations, see 10.36–8).

Rate rebate

5.80 The rating authority is under a duty to provide rate rebates to occupiers of hereditaments under certain circumstances. All normal rate liability, valuation and procedural rules are observed, but in its rate demand, the rate authority is empowered to give rate rebates in the following cases.

Housing benefits

5.81 Rating rebates are now dealt together with rent rebates and rent allowances, generally referred to as *housing benefits*, under Part II of the Social Security and Housing Benefits Act 1982.

5.82 Under the *statutory rate rebate scheme* rate rebates are now treated by rating authorities in one of two ways:

(a) Certificated rate rebates: a certificate from the Department of Health and Social Security informs the rating authority of those people who receive social security payments and who, in addition, qualify for rate rebates. The rating authority will credit such individuals with the full amount of rates otherwise payable. However, less than full rates due will be credited if, for example, there is a non-dependent adult living in the dwelling together with the rateable occupier.

(b) Standard rate rebate: the standard rate rebate is given to a rateable occupier who does not qualify for social security payments but who, nevertheless, is entitled to a rate rebate because of low income. The standard rate rebate is calculated by the rating authority every half year on the basis of weekly income against the statutory needs allowance.

5.83 The Secretary of State is required to review the needs allowances each year to ascertain if they have retained their value in relation to prices and housing costs. He must either produce regulations to increase the allowances as appropriate, or provide a report explaining to Parliament his reasons for not doing so.

5.84 Although there is a statutory requirement to provide a rate rebate scheme, rating authorities may introduce a *local rate rebate scheme* if they decide to vary the statutory scheme. A local scheme is subject to safeguards which ensure that no one receives a lower rebate than if the statutory scheme operated, and that the total cost of the scheme shall not exceed a 'permitted total' of rebates and allowances.

Disabled persons

5.85 The Rating (Disabled Persons) Act 1978 provides a detailed framework by which rebates are granted for occupiers whose *dwelling-houses* have been *structurally adapted or constructed to provide special facilities for the disabled*.

5.86 The *special facilities* are an additional room, bathroom, heating, floor space for a wheelchair, garage, carport, hard-standing for a vehicle or any other facility. The special facilities must be '. . . essential or of major importance to [the disabled person's] wellbeing by reason of the nature and extent of his disability'.

5.87 No rebate can be granted except by application to the rating authority and, if the applicant qualifies, the relief is mandatory.

5.88 The amount of the rebate is determined under s 1 of the 1978 Act, and is equal to the amount of rates attributable to the special feature (eg £30 rateable value is attributable to a room, other than a bathroom).

5.89 However, under s 1, para 11(1), 'the valuation officer shall certify what amount of rateable value is . . . attributed . . . and his certificate shall be conclusive'. But there is no duty on the rating authority to refer an application to the valuation officer for his consideration.

5.90 There is an appeal to the local valuation court against any valuation officer's certificate.

5.91 The 1978 Act allows an appeal to the county court against the rating authority's refusal of an application for a rebate (although apparently no appeal exists if a rebate granted is less than that to which the applicant thinks he is entitled). .

5.92 *Rebates for institutions* for the disabled are covered by s 2, under which '. . . the rating authority . . . shall grant a rebate in respect of rates chargeable on any hereditament . . . which is occupied by a local authority or other body and is used . . .' wholly or partly for:

   (a) residential accommodation for care and after-care of persons suffering from illness;
   (b) training or keeping suitably occupied persons suffering from illness;
   (c) providing like accommodation (as above) for disabled persons;
   (d) providing welfare structures for disabled persons;
   (e) providing facilities for employment under the Disabled Persons (Employment) Acts 1944 and 1958.

5.93 The rebate granted is equal to the rates chargeable on the hereditament. If relief is also available under s 40, for charitable and other similar organisations, the section operates as if the rates paid under it are reduced by the rebate granted by the Rating (Disabled Persons) Act 1978.

5.94 Under s 8(1), a disabled person is any person who is blind, deaf or dumb, or who suffers from mental disorder of any description or who is substantially and permanently handicapped by illness, injury or congenital deformity or any other disability prescribed for the purposes of the National Assistance Act 1948.

Reduction of the rate in the pound

5.95 The rate in the pound is fixed annually by the rating authority having regard to its financial needs, as well as those of the authorities which precept on it.

5.96 Under s 48, a reduction in the rate in the pound is given to all occupiers of *residential accommodation*, whether assessed as a separate hereditament or part of a larger hereditament, part of which is used for non-residential purposes (called a *mixed hereditament*).

5.97 The rate in the pound applied to the rateable value of domestic property is that rate which is fixed by the rating authority but reduced by a 'prescribed amount' (currently 18.5p in England and Wales).

5.98 Thus, with a rate in the pound fixed at 208.7p in a given rating area, the rate poundage actually applied to the rateable values of dwellings in that area is 190.2p.

5.99 The loss in revenue to the rating authority is made up by central government grants.

5.100 Initially, it is sufficient that a hereditament should appear to the rating authority to be a *mixed hereditament*. The procedure set out in the Mixed Hereditaments (Certificate) Regulations 1967 may be used to appeal against the refusal of the rating authority to treat the hereditament as a mixed hereditament.

5.101 Where a rating authority *refuses* or is deemed to have refused to treat a hereditament as a mixed hereditament, the occupier of the hereditament may apply to the valuation officer for a certificate stating whether or not it is a mixed hereditament. The valuation officer sends a copy of the certificate to the applicant and the rating authority, who both have the right of objection, in which case the matter is decided by the local valuation court.

5.102 In the case of a *mixed hereditament*, the amount of the reduction will depend on the ratio of the value of residential use to the total rateable value.

5.103 Where the ratio of residential use is more than half the total rateable value, a reduction of half the standard amount is given; where the ratio is between half and a quarter, the reduction is a quarter of the standard amount; if the ratio is between a quarter and one-eighth, the reduction is one-eighth of the standard amount. There is no reduction in the rate in the pound if the proportion of residential value to total rateable value is less than one-eighth.

5.104 Thus, in 1986/87, the Vale of Glamorgan Borough Council give the following rate reductions to a rate in the pound of 208.7p:

	Reduction	Rate in the £
Where the property is used wholly for domestic purposes	18.5p	190.2
Where the domestic use accounts for more than half the total rateable value	9.2p	199.5
Where the domestic use accounts for more than a quarter but not more than half the total rateable value	4.6p	204.1
Where the domestic use accounts for more than an eighth but not more than a quarter of the total rateable value	2.3p	206.4

Net annual value does not equal rateable value (derating)

5.105 In the majority of cases, rateable value is the same as net annual value. Rateable value is the figure which, when multiplied by the rate in the pound, produces the rates payable. Net annual value is the net annual rental value of a hereditament, calculated using the normal methods of valuation (see Chapters 7 and 9).

5.106 However, in rare circumstances, net annual value is not the same as rateable value, in which case the normal rate burden is not borne by the ratepayer. This is known as derating. This method of giving rate relief has, in the past, been applied to industrial hereditaments—see Appendix 1.

Mines and quarries

5.107 The Mines and Quarries (Valuation) Order 1983 provides that the net annual value of a *mine* or *quarry* shall be reduced by half the rent attributable to the land (excluding buildings or other items) in order to arrive at the rateable value of the hereditament. This reduction recognises that, in paying a mineral royalty, half is rent and half payment for the mineral extracted and, as such, should be treated as capital.

Future valuation lists: specified and unspecified hereditaments

5.108 Under s 30 of the LGPLA 1980, the Secretary of State has power to specify the types of hereditaments which are to be revalued for a future valuation list. Hereditaments which are not specified will not be revalued, instead their existing net annual values will be '*adjusted by any method prescribed*'; thus net annual values for unspecified hereditaments will not equal rateable values.

5.109 There is a requirement on the Secretary of State to 'preserve the ratio which he estimates will exist . . . between the rateable values of specified hereditaments in England and Wales as a whole and the rateable values of unspecified hereditaments in England and Wales as a whole'.

5.110 Any artificial calculation of rateable value is likely to result in an artificial distribution of the rate burden. The requirement of the Secretary of State to preserve 'the ratio' which exists between the rateable values of specified and unspecified hereditaments in England and Wales involves a ratio of values based on a national average to be estimated and maintained. Reassessing local differences in rate burden, which would be fairly maintained on the basis of rental value if a full revaluation were to be carried out, will not occur.

5.111 Should these provisions be used for a new valuation list, it is obvious that while, nationally, the burden of rates will be shared between specified and unspecified hereditaments at the same ratio after new lists come into force as before, on a parish or even regional basis, this is unlikely to be the case.

Alteration of statutory deductions

5.112 When certain property (eg a house) is valued for rating purposes, a gross value must be found. In order to convert a gross value to a net annual value, an amount known as 'statutory deductions' is subtracted from the gross value.

5.113 Thus, gross value less statutory deductions equals net annual value (see 7.11–26).

5.114 Statutory deductions represent outgoings for repairs etc, but instead of being valued for each property, they are laid down in the Valuation (Statutory Deductions) Order 1973 (see 7.25).

5.115 The amount of the statutory deductions is fixed by the amount of the gross value, regardless of the type or nature of the hereditament—a totally artificial means of arriving at an amount to represent outgoings.

5.116 It follows, therefore, that for some properties, an increase or decrease in statutory deductions will give a greater or lesser rate liability with no apparent increase or decrease in rental value.

5.117 The last occasion on which statutory deductions were altered was with effect from 1 April 1974, as a result of which the rateable values of hereditaments with low gross values (between £55 and £330) were marginally reduced.

Checklist

5.118 Agricultural land, defined as arable, meadow or pasture land, is exempt from rates if solely used for these purposes.

5.119 Agricultural buildings (not a dwellinghouse) must generally be occupied with agricultural land and used solely in connection with agricultural operations on that land to be exempt from rates. The definition includes buildings used for intensive raising of livestock, keeping bees, buildings occupied by certain corporate bodies and fish farm buildings.

5.120 Parks and pleasure grounds run by a local authority are treated as not in beneficial occupation.

5.121 Churches, ie places of public religious worship, are exempt from rates. Church halls etc occupied with a place of worship are exempt. Lettings at a profit will cause exemption to be lost for one year.

5.122 In enterprise zones, hereditaments which are neither dwelling-houses nor public utility hereditaments are exempt.

5.123 'Mothballed' factories which are unused but contain plant and machinery are not rateable.

5.124 Miscellaneous exemptions: lighthouses, buoys and beacons; sewers, manholes, pumping stations etc; drainage authorities' land structures or appliances; air raid protection works; rooms used for elections.

5.125 The Crown, including servants of the Crown, is exempt from rates on hereditaments it occupies. Any occupation for the purposes of government is Crown occupation and, therefore, exempt. The Crown makes a contribution in lieu of rates.

5.126 Foreign sovereigns and diplomats are exempt from rates.

5.127 Rating authorities grant relief to charities and similar organis-ations by giving:

    (a) mandatory relief of half rates payable—to registered charities;
    (b) discretionary relief available to registered charities and other non-profit-making organisations.

5.128 In cases of poverty, rates are remitted on the grounds of hardship.

5.129 Agricultural dwellinghouses—gross value is assessed assuming the dwelling is available only for occupation by agricultural workers.

5.130 Dwellinghouses—no proposal may be made for an increase in gross value because of structural alterations after 1 April 1974 either for the addition of central heating or for any alteration which increases the gross value by more than £30.

5.131 Rate rebates are given to residential occupiers on low incomes, and to disabled persons where rebates relate to special facilities which are essential or of major importance to the wellbeing of the disabled person. There are also rebates for institutions for the disabled.

5.132 A reduction in the rate in the pound is applied to dwellinghouses and a portion of that reduction is applied to the dwelling part of a mixed hereditament.

5.133 Net annual value does not equal rateable value for mines and quarries, neither is it likely that net annual value will equal rateable value for 'unspecified hereditaments' on a future revaluation.

5.134 Alteration of statutory deductions can affect the rate liability for properties which are valued to gross value.

Chapter 6

Rating of owners

Synopsis

6.1 Rates is an occupiers' tax. Owners pay rates in their capacity as occupiers.

6.2 However, there are occasions when statute makes owners liable for rates in their capacity as owners.

6.3 There may be an occupier who would, under different circumstances, pay rates or there may not be an occupier.

6.4 It is usual for an owner who is liable to pay rates to be able to propose alterations to and appeal against the assessment as if he were an occupier.

Rationale

6.5 Owners often pay rates in their capacity as occupiers, but there are occasions when owners become liable for rates on property which they do not occupy.

6.6 In the case of *empty property*, provisions exist to rate owners, quite contrary to the principles of rateable occupation. Society accepts it to be equitable that owners of property which benefit from services provided by the local authority should contribute towards this provision. Rating law was altered to meet this change of attitude in the Local Government Act 1966.

6.7 Rating law has been altered again to *facilitate rate collection* for the rating authority. By making the owner responsible for rate payment, either by altering the hereditament from several to one, or by just making the owner a 'go-between', rate collection becomes more certain and, therefore, cheaper for everyone.

6.8   Rating has even been used to *punish* owners who (apparently) deliberately keep commercial property empty, by using rates as a surcharge to discourage the practice.

Compounding

6.9   Compounding generally occurs when a property is occupied by a tenant, and involves making the owner responsible for rates in substitution for the occupier. This can be achieved either compulsorily or by agreement.

6.10   The statutory provisions which relate to compounding are found in ss 55 and 56.

6.11   *Compulsory compounding* (s 55(1)) forces an owner to be liable for rates instead of the occupier. The rating authority may pass a resolution directing that the owners (instead of occupiers) of all hereditaments in its area which belong to a specific class shall be rated. This class is defined by reference to rateable value (which must not exceed £200). If rent is paid, the rating authority may also define the class by reference to the intervals at which rent is paid.

6.12   In such cases, a rating authority may by resolution determine, a discount of 10 per cent (or such proportion as the rating authority may determine) is granted (LGPLA 1980, s 36(2)).

6.13   A direction given under s 55 may be rescinded, but the rescinding resolution takes effect only at the end of the rate period.

6.14   The allowance paid to owners who are compulsorily compounded is only made if the rates are paid promptly within specified time limits.

6.15   *Voluntary compounding* (s 56(1)): rating authorities are empowered to enter into an agreement with the owner of any hereditament where the rent is payable or collected at intervals shorter than quarterly (ie weekly, monthly etc). In this case, there is no rateable value limit fixed.

6.16   By such an agreement, an owner may undertake either:

(a) to pay rates chargeable whether the property is occupied or not, in which case the rating authority may agree to a discount not exceeding 10 per cent;

(b) to pay rates chargeable only so long as the property is occupied, when a maximum allowance of 7.5 per cent may be agreed;

(c) to collect the rates due from the occupier and pay them to the rating authority, when the maximum allowance is 5 per cent.

6.17 These percentage allowances may be varied by the rating authority which, by resolution, may determine a different allowance in each case (LGPLA 1980, s 36(5) and (6)). The allowances are only made if the amount due is paid on or before the dates specified in the agreement.

6.18 Any agreement may be terminated by notice given either by the rating authority or the owner (s 56(3)); the notice has the effect of ending the agreement on the last day of the next complete rate period.

6.19 An agreement entered into by one owner will continue to be binding on succeeding owners, until determined as above.

6.20 Where the owner agrees merely to collect the rates on behalf of the rating authority (see 6.16(c)), the amount due from the owner may not necessarily be the whole amount of the rate (less any discount). If the owner has actually collected only part of the aggregate of rent and rates due from the tenant, the amount of rates to be paid is calculated according to the proportion which the aggregate amount collected bears to the aggregate amount due.

6.21 Whether an owner is rated compulsorily under s 55(1) or voluntarily under s 56(1), unpaid rates may be recovered from him in the same manner as unpaid rates are recovered from an occupier, ie by distress (seizure of goods).

6.22 Under s 58, an occupier of a hereditament let to him for a term not exceeding three months is not to be compelled to pay more than a quarter's rates at a time.

6.23 If an owner who is rated omits or neglects to pay the rating authority, the occupier may pay the rates and deduct them from the rent due (s 59).

6.24 Also, at any time while rates remain unpaid by the owner, the rating authority may recover them by distress from the occupier, provided the rates are demanded from the occupier in writing and he has not paid them within fourteen days of the service of the demand, and further that no greater sum is raised than is actually due from the occupier as rates of the property. The occupier may deduct the amount levied and the expenses of distress from the rent due to the owner.

6.25 For the purposes of ss 50 (payment of rates by instalments), 55 and 56, s 115(1) defines an 'owner' as '. . . a person who is . . . entitled to receive the rent payable . . .'.

6.26 In relation to any right of appeal, either to the county court against a rate or to the local valuation court for the purposes of objections, proposals and appeals relating to a valuation list, an owner rated under s 55(1) is entitled to be treated as standing in the same position as the occupier, without prejudice to the rights of the occupier (ss 57(2) and 81(2)).

House adapted for occupation in parts

6.27   Where a dwelling or the dwelling part of a building is occupied in parts, under s 24 the valuation officer has the discretion either to assess that building or part in the normal way (as several hereditaments) or as one hereditament in the occupation of the owner.

6.28   The phrase 'occupied in parts' must mean rateably occupied and the section only applies where there are separate occupations as determined by normal rating rules.

6.29   The section applies only:

> where a building which was constructed or has been adapted (a) for the purposes of a single dwelling or (b) as to part thereof for such purposes and as to the remainder thereof for any purpose other than that of a dwelling, is occupied in parts.

6.30   The discretion is exercised 'having regard to all the circumstances of the case, including the extent, if any, to which the parts separately occupied have been severed by structural alterations' (s 24).

6.31   Where it is decided to assess a house (or the dwelling part of a property) as a 'house adapted for occupation in parts', it 'shall, for the purposes of rating, be deemed to be a single hereditament in the occupation of the person who receives the rents payable in respect of the parts' (s 24).

6.32   The discretion applies to a single dwelling, either purpose-built or adapted for such domestic use, and to the dwelling part of a single dwelling with business premises attached to it, eg shop with dwelling-house over it. It does not apply where a house has been purpose-built as two or more dwellings.

6.33   It is usual to find the section applied to houses which comprise non-self-contained flat units (the degree of severance was specifically mentioned as a criterion to be considered), and where the owner is not resident.

6.34   Where a proposal is made to have such a house either rated as a single hereditament or as several hereditaments, the court has no authority to substitute its decision for the discretion of the valuation officer as to whether or not a property is occupied in parts. The court can only consider whether all the conditions precedent to the exercise of the discretion have been fulfilled, and whether the valuation officer has had 'regard to all the circumstances of the case' (*Lewis-Jones* v *Williams (VO) and Cardiff City Council* (1970)).

6.35   Any owner rated under these provisions is the rateable occupier for the purposes of making and objecting to a proposal in relation to that house adapted for occupation in parts.

Empty properties

6.36   Owners may become liable to rates as a result of the rating of unoccupied properties. The power to rate empty properties (first given to rating authorities by the Local Government Act 1966) is covered by s 17 and Sched 1 and is a significant development in a tax traditionally linked to occupation.

6.37   The decision to rate unoccupied property belongs to the individual rating authority, which may resolve to bring the necessary provisions into effect, or make those provisions cease to have effect. A rating authority may resolve that only particular classes of unoccupied property shall be rated, but has no discretion regarding individual unoccupied properties.

6.38   The provisions always take effect on the first day of a rate period and cease to apply on the last day of a rate period (s 17(2)).

6.39   Once the resolution has brought the necessary provisions of s 17(1) into effect, liability to be rated in respect of unoccupied property attaches to owners (ie the person entitled to possession) of the 'relevant hereditaments' (Sched 1, para 1(1)), defined in para 15 as

> . . . consisting of, or of any part of, a house, shop, office, factory, mill or other building, together with any garden, yard, court or other land ordinarily used or intended for use for the purposes of the building or part.

6.40   The hereditament must have been unoccupied for a continuous period exceeding three months or such longer period as the Secretary of State may by order specify (LGPLA 1980, s 42). Where the hereditament has been unoccupied and then becomes occupied for a period of less than six weeks, for the purposes of calculating the three-month period, that period of less than six weeks' occupation is treated as non-occupation.

6.41   If the property is a *dwellinghouse*, these provisions apply, but the period of non-occupation is increased to six months or such longer period as the Secretary of State may by order specify (LGPLA 1980, s 42).

6.42 The provisions for rating empty property apply as if the hereditament were occupied by the owner, and the amount of rates he pays is the proportion of rates specified by the rating authority in its resolution.

6.43 From 1 April 1981 a ceiling of 50 per cent rates was placed on the charge which could be levied on empty commercial and industrial property.

6.44 An owner of unoccupied hereditaments is not liable to pay rates on property which is empty because (Sched 1, para 2(a)–(f)):

(a) he is prohibited by law from occupying or allowing the hereditament to be occupied;

(b) the hereditament is kept vacant because either the Crown or the local authority intends prohibiting occupation, or acquiring it;

(c) the hereditament is the subject of a building preservation notice (Town and Country Planning Act 1971, s 58) or has been designated as a building of architectural or historical interest;

(d) the hereditament is the subject of a preservation notice under the Ancient Monuments Acts 1913 to 1953;

(e) there is an agreement in force under s 56(1)—voluntary compounding;

(f) the hereditament is held for the purpose of being available for occupation by a minister of religion as a residence from which to perform his duties.

6.45 There are six other exemptions made by the Secretary of State in the Rating (Exemption of Unoccupied Property) Regulations 1967 (SI 1967 No 954), reg 2(a)–(f). These basically refer to the status of the owner, eg if he is entitled to possession in his capacity as a personal representative of a deceased person, as a trustee under a deed of arrangement, or as a liquidator under the Companies Act 1985.

6.46 The rating authority may reduce or remit the payment of rates on unoccupied property if it is considered that it will cause hardship to the person liable (Sched 1, para 1(3A)).

6.47 As a direct result of the current economic recession, and the aim of central government to encourage industry, the Secretary of State has introduced regulations suspending the powers of the rating authority to levy rates on certain empty hereditaments with effect from 1 April 1986. These must previously have been used for a trade or business which involves the manufacture and/or storage of goods, or the processing of minerals, but excludes retail premises (Rating (Exemption of Unoccupied Industrial and Storage Hereditaments) Regulations 1985). (So-called 'mothballed' factories are exempt under s 46A—see 5.32–4.)

Properties recently constructed

6.48 A rating authority may request the valuation officer to make a proposal for including in the current valuation list any unoccupied building which is or will be a *newly constructed dwellinghouse*. If the valuation officer is prepared to comply, he will make a proposal to include that building in the list and give it the value considered appropriate when the building is completed. Once the value appears in the valuation list, rates are payable by the owner.

6.49 If the valuation officer informs the rating authority that he does not propose to assess the building, the rating authority may make a proposal to include that building in the list as a dwellinghouse and to ascribe to it the value it considers appropriate when the building is complete. This is the only occasion when someone other than a valuation officer can propose that a hereditament be entered into the valuation list for the first time (see 12.11).

6.50 Any person liable to be rated in respect of such a hereditament is treated as being in the same position as the occupier of the hereditament in relation to proposals, objections and appeals (Sched 1, para 11(11)).

6.51 In the case of any *other new buildings*, a rating authority has power to serve a *completion notice* on the owner where it is of the opinion that the construction works have been completed, or that the work remaining to be done is such that it can reasonably be expected to be completed within three months (Sched 1, para 8(1)).

6.52 The completion notice states that the building will be treated as complete on the date specified in the notice, after which time the three-month period of non-occupation will run (see 6.40), after which time the owner is liable for rates. An appeal against the completion notice lies to the county court.

Rating surcharge on unused commercial property

6.53 The principle of the rating of unoccupied property was greatly extended by the Local Government Act 1974, the provisions of which have been suspended by the Rating Surcharge (Suspension) Order 1980 with effect from 1 April 1981.

6.54 Under s 16 of the Local Government Act 1974 (which inserts ss 17A and 17B into the GRA 1967), the owner (ie the person entitled to possession) of a commercial building which, for a continuous period exceeding six months, is not used for the purpose for which it was constructed or adapted, had to pay a surcharge in respect of the 'period of non-use', in addition to the rates otherwise payable.

6.55 A commercial building is a hereditament which is not a dwelling-house or lock-up garage with a floor space of less than 240 square feet (22.29 square metres), the net annual value of which is ascertained by calculating a gross value and deducting statutory deductions (see Chapter 7).

6.56 The surcharge was not payable if:

(a) the building was unfit for the purpose for which it was constructed or adapted and could not be rendered fit at a reasonable cost (s 17A(2)(*a*)); or

(b) the owner had tried his best to let the building (s 17A(5)).

6.57 The surcharge was levied in the form of rates, by doubling the normal rates for the first twelve months of non-use, trebling for the second twelve months and so on; it became a charge on the land until recovered.

6.58 There were several exemptions from the surcharge provisions which have been suspended with effect from 1 April 1981 (Rating Surcharge (Suspension) Order 1980). They remain, however, within the GRA 1967 and could be invoked again if the Secretary of State makes the appropriate order.

Checklist

6.59 Compulsory compounding forces an owner to be liable for rates instead of the occupier.

6.60 Voluntary compounding allows the rating authority and the owner to agree that the owner will either:

(a) pay the rates whether the property is occupied or not;

(b) pay the rates while the property is occupied; or

(c) collect the rates due from the occupier and transmit them to the rating authority.

6.61 A house adapted for occupation in parts may be a single hereditament in the rateable occupation of the owner.

6.62 Rating authorities have discretion to rate empty properties in their area, the rates being paid by the owners, after six weeks' non-occupation.

6.63 In the case of an empty dwellinghouse, the period of non-occupation prior to rates being paid is six months.

6.64 The maximum rates which can be levied on empty commercial and industrial property is 50 per cent.

6.65 The above powers are suspended in respect of unoccupied industrial and storage hereditaments.

6.66 Recently constructed unoccupied dwellings must be the subject of a proposal—made either by the valuation officer or the rating authority—and an entry in the valuation list before rates can be levied.

6.67 Recently constructed unoccupied non-domestic property is subject to a completion notice served by the rating authority before rates can be levied.

6.68 The provisions which imposed a surcharge on unused commercial properties have been suspended.

Chapter 7

Basis of assessment

Synopsis

7.1 Rates are a tax on the value of the occupation of land. The value of the occupation on which rates are paid is rateable value. Thus, rateable value × rates in £ = rates paid.

7.2 Generally, rateable value equals net annual value. A net annual value must be fixed for all hereditaments.

7.3 However, net annual value can be found in two ways, depending on the type of hereditament involved. Either:

(a) a hereditament is valued direct to net annual value; or
(b) a hereditament is valued to gross value, from which a sum is deducted for outgoings, to arrive at net annual value. In this case, gross value less statutory deductions equals net annual value.

7.4 In both cases a rent must be found, assuming a tenancy the conditions of which have been established by case law.

Net annual value

7.5 The basis of assessment is net annual value, and (with the exception of mineral-producing hereditaments) the rateable value on which rates are paid is the same as net annual value.

7.6 Net annual value can be fixed in two ways, either by direct calculation or by calculating a gross value and deducting statutory deductions.

7.7 It is the nature of the hereditament which will govern the method of assessing net annual value.

63

7.8   Section 19(2) states that *gross value must be found* for any hereditament 'consisting of one or more *houses or other non-industrial buildings*, with or without any garden, yard, court, forecourt, outhouse, or other appurtenance belonging thereto, but *without other land*'.

7.9   Thus, for houses and other non-industrial buildings without other land (ie shops, offices, hotels etc, including warehouses) net annual value is gross value less statutory deductions. ('House' includes part of a house.) (See also 7.19–21.)

7.10   Section 19(3) states that *in all other cases net annual value is to be ascertained direct*.

7.11   *Gross value* is defined in s 19(6) as being:

> the rent at which the hereditament might reasonably be expected to let from year to year if the tenant undertook to pay all usual tenant's rates and taxes and the landlord undertook to bear the cost of the repairs and insurance and the other expenses, if any, necessary to maintain the hereditament in a state to command that rent.

7.12   Gross value is therefore an annual rent, with the landlord bearing all outgoings except tenant's rates.

7.13   In order to arrive at a net annual value from gross value, a scale of outgoings, called *statutory deductions*, is produced by central government, so that gross value less statutory deductions equals net annual value (see 7.25).

7.14   In cases where *net annual value* is ascertained directly, it is defined in s 19(3) as:

> an amount equal to the rent at which it is estimated the hereditament might reasonably be expected to let from year to year if the tenant undertook to pay all usual tenant's rates and taxes and to bear the cost of the repairs and insurance and the other expenses, if any, necessary to maintain the hereditament in a state to command that rent.

7.15   Net annual value is, therefore, an annual rent with the tenant bearing all outgoings.

7.16   The essential difference is that gross value assumes that outgoings are the landlord's responsibility, while in net annual value they are the tenant's responsibility.

7.17   It is important to assess properties according to these definitions. It has been held illegal (*Sandown Park Ltd* v *Esher UDC and Castle*

(VO) (1954)) to arrive at gross value by adding back statutory deductions to net annual value.

7.18   Thus, gross value must be arrived at for houses and non-industrial buildings with or without appurtenances but without other land.

7.19   With regard to 'any garden, yard, court, forecourt, outhouse or other appurtenance belonging thereto', *appurtenance* is undefined. What seems likely from case law is that under a conveyance of a property, an 'appurtenance' will pass without actually being mentioned.

7.20   Thus, if a property includes land and non-industrial buildings, and on a conveyance of the property the land would pass without being mentioned, the land is appurtenant to the buildings and the property requires a gross value (*Clymo (VO)* v *Shell-Mex and BP Ltd* (1963)). If this is not the case, the land is 'other land' and the property requires a net annual value calculated directly.

7.21   For dwellinghouses and educational establishments, s 19(6) defines 'appurtenance' as including 'all land occupied' with the building 'and used for the purposes thereof' and will include a garden, garage, garden shed etc.

7.22   *Non-industrial buildings* is defined in s 19(6) to mean:

a building or part of a building of any description other than:

(a) factories, mills and other premises of a similar character used wholly or mainly for industrial purposes; or
(b) premises forming part, and taken into account in the valuation for rating purposes, of:
  (i) a railway, dock, canal, gas, water or electricity undertaking; or
  (ii) any public utility undertaking, not falling within sub-paragraph (i) . . .

(There is no definition of 'public utility undertaking'.)

7.23   Note that with this very narrow definition of industrial buildings, such properties as warehouses are non-industrial buildings.

7.24   For dwellings and other non-industrial hereditaments without other land, therefore, net annual value can be calculated by first ascertaining gross value and deducting from that the *statutory deductions*, to give net annual value.

7.25   The statutory instrument in force is the Valuation (Statutory Deductions) Order 1973 (made under s 19(2)). Five levels of deduction are laid down depending on the gross value of the hereditament:

Gross value	Deductions from gross value
Not exceeding £65	45%
Exceeding £65 not exceeding £128	£29 + 30% of GV in excess of £65
Exceeding £128 not exceeding £330	£48 + 66 $2/3$% of GV in excess of £128
Exceeding £330 not exceeding £430	£80 + 20% of GV in excess of £330
Exceeding £430	£100 + 16 $2/3$% of GV in excess of £430

7.26 This scale is intended to cover the cost of repairs, insurance etc which under gross value is the landlord's responsibility, but the amount of the deduction is related only to the amount of the gross value. The factors which affect the amount spent on outgoings, such as type of property, age, condition etc are irrelevant to the amount of the deduction.

7.27 Generally the rateable value of a hereditament is the same as the net annual value. In the past, there were hereditaments with rateable values which differed from net annual values (see Chapter 5 and Appendix 1). However, as from 1 April 1971 the rateable value of certain hereditaments to which the Mines and Quarries (Valuation) Order 1983 applies are less than their net annual values (see 5.105–7).

7.28 It is not proposed to discuss further the provisions relating to mines etc. It is considered sufficient in this text to say that they are subject to different rules and tend to be specialised items to value and assess to rates (the Bibliography lists more detailed texts).

Hypothetical tenancy

7.29 As has been pointed out (7.16), the only difference between the statutory definitions of gross value and net annual value is that in the former the landlord has the burden of 'repairs and insurance, and the expenses necessary to maintain the hereditament in a state to command that rent', and in the latter they are the tenant's responsibility.

7.30 Both definitions require that a *rent* be found. Rent is only paid under a tenancy agreement, and so such a tenancy agreement must be assumed. In fact, this hypothetical tenancy must be assumed each time a property is valued to either gross value or net annual value.

7.31 It is not possible to fix a rent under the statutory definitions without making such an assumption, and although the hypothetical tenancy is not mentioned in any statute, case law has expanded its terms beyond those laid down in the statutory definitions.

7.32 Because the hypothetical tenancy must be assumed, there must also be assumed a hypothetical tenant to pay the rent, and a hypothetical landlord to receive it.

7.33 A tenant and landlord may or may not actually exist for the property, but they are almost irrelevant for rating purposes.

7.34 In every case, a hypothetical tenancy, tenant and landlord must be assumed, whether a property is owner-occupied, held on a building lease, a three-year lease or occupied illegally (title is, of course, irrelevant—see Chapter 2).

7.35 In fixing a gross or net annual value, it is necessary to find the *rent* at which the property would let. It is therefore necessary to ignore the fact that it is occupied and to imagine, *if the property were vacant* and available for letting, what annual rental figure the hypothetical tenant would offer, bearing in mind the responsibility for outgoings.

7.36 All potential *occupiers* of the hereditament must be considered as possible hypothetical tenants. These will include the owner-occupier, any actual tenant and an actual landlord.

7.37 It may not be factually or legally possible for the actual occupier to be a tenant of a hereditament. Nevertheless, for the purpose of valuing that hereditament for rating, it must be assumed that the actual occupier is among the possible yearly tenants (*R* v *School Board for London* (1886)).

7.38 An owner of property which is in fact let to another is also a possible hypothetical tenant, and the *owner's rental bid* must be considered in fixing the rental value under the statutory definitions (*Davies* v *Seisdon Union* (1908)).

7.39 The rent to be estimated is *the rent which might reasonably be expected*. This is not the actual rent paid or the legally demandable rent for the hereditament. The hereditament is to be considered 'let from year to year' and not for a term of years. However, it must be assumed that there is a *reasonable prospect of continuance*, and the 'year to year' rent must be calculated on that basis.

7.40 The impact of all foreseeable events on the rent paid under the hypothetical tenancy must be taken into account (*Dawkins (VO)* v *Ash Bros and Heaton Ltd* (1969)). Some proposed events will not affect an annual rental bid until a much later date (*Lloyd (VO)* v *Rossleigh Ltd* (1962)); other events may affect capital values but not rental values, and will not therefore affect the rating assessments.

7.41 Although most anticipated events will affect the rent, they will not always affect the gross or net annual value because of the hypothetical nature of the assumed tenancy.

7.42 Thus, where the occupation will be terminated in less than a year as a result of some action beyond the control of the actual landlord and tenant, and such a prospect affects the value of the occupation, the gross or net annual value is reduced by the prospect of the termination (*Dawkins (VO)* v *Ash Bros and Heaton Ltd* (1969)).

7.43 This would not be true if the actual landlord intended to demolish for his own reasons, because the hypothetical landlord is the one involved in the hypothetical tenancy. In such a case, the assessment would not be reduced, but a full year's rates would not be paid if occupation did not last twelve months (*Burley (VO)* v *A & W Birch Ltd* (1959)).

7.44 In normal cases, any question as to the actual tenant's *ability to pay* a rent must be disregarded, because it is always the rental bid of the hypothetical tenant which is needed. However, where the demand for a particular hereditament is very restricted, and especially where there is only one hypothetical tenant, ability to pay is taken into account. This point has been applied to the assessments of football grounds, cricket clubs and certain Oxford colleges.

7.45 Tenant's rates and taxes will now only include (general) rates and will not include land drainage rates or special rates. (A 'water rate' as a charge for water supplied is always payable by a tenant, just as an electricity or gas bill.)

7.46 Under the definition of net annual value, the tenant bears the cost of *repairs*, insurance and the other expenses necessary to maintain the hereditament in a state to command that rent. If the hereditament requires a gross value, these costs are the landlord's responsibility and a statutory deduction is made to allow for the cost of those outgoings to produce a net annual value. In the statutory definition this obligation to repair includes internal decorations and the obligation to put the premises into repair if that is necessary (*Wexler* v *Playle (VO)* (1960)).

7.47 Drainage rates, sea defence rates, fishing rates and similar charges on the owner are 'expenses necessary to maintain the hereditament in a state to command that rent', and such expenses can include expenditure on other land if it is necessary to preserve the physical existence of the hereditament.

Future valuation lists (see also 11.19–26)

7.48 As from the date on which new valuation lists come into force (under s 28 LGPLA 1980, a new list will come into force when the Secretary of State specifies, the order receiving parliamentary approval), there will be a new basis for the valuation of non-domestic, non-industrial buildings.

7.49 As from the date when new lists come into force, a *gross value* will be required *only* for 'a dwellinghouse, a private garage or private storage premises' (s 29), ie *domestic hereditaments*.

7.50 *All other hereditaments previously valued to gross value will be valued direct to net annual value*.

7.51 Thus, once the Secretary of State makes an order, approved by Parliament, that new valuation lists shall come into force, the only hereditaments which will be valued to gross value will be dwelling-houses, private garages and private storage premises (see 7.56). These will be the only hereditaments for which gross value must be estimated and to which statutory deductions must be applied to arrive at net annual value.

7.52 For all other hereditaments (with the exception of those valued by statutory formulae) net annual value must be calculated directly, in accordance with the statutory definition (s 19(3)—see 7.14).

7.53 For all future valuation lists, therefore, commercial property including shops and offices will have rating assessments calculated on a net annual value—far more realistic since much of such property which is rented is let on net (full repairing and insuring) terms.

7.54 Not only is this basis more realistic as far as the market is concerned, but market evidence of rental values can be more easily and more accurately applied to valuations for rating purposes.

7.55 Section 29(4) of the LGPLA 1980 gives the Secretary of State power to make regulations giving transitional relief to ratepayers liable to higher rates as a result of this change in valuation basis.

7.56 For the purposes of a future valuation list, a private garage is defined as 'a building having a floor area not exceeding 25 square metres and used wholly or mainly for the accommodation of a motor vehicle'. Private storage premises are defined as 'a hereditament which is used wholly in conjunction with a dwellinghouse or dwellinghouses and used wholly or mainly for the storage of articles of domestic use (including bicycles and similar vehicles) belonging to persons residing there'.

7.57 *These provisions are not yet in force*, but will take effect when the new valuation lists, due 1 April 1990, are introduced.

Checklist

7.58   Rates levied = rateable value × rate in £.

7.59   Rateable value equals net annual value (s 19).

7.60   Net annual value for houses and non-industrial buildings without other land is gross value less statutory deductions (Valuation (Statutory Deductions) Order 1973).

7.61   Gross value is required for '. . . houses and other non-industrial buildings . . . without other land', and is defined (s 19(6)) as the rent at which the hereditament might reasonably be expected to let from year to year if the tenant undertook to pay all usual tenant's rates and taxes and the landlord undertook to bear the cost of repairs and insurance etc.

7.62   Net annual value is required for all other hereditaments, and is defined (s 19(3)) as an amount equal to the rent at which it is estimated the hereditament might reasonably be expected to let from year to year if the tenant undertook to pay all usual tenant's rates and taxes and to bear the cost of the repairs and insurance etc.

7.63   A hypothetical tenancy is assumed for both gross value and net annual value definitions. Case law enlarges the terms of the hypothetical tenancy:

(a) hereditament must be considered available for letting;
(b) the rent (gross/net annual value) to be fixed is the rent which a hypothetical tenant would pay for the property under the terms of the statutory definitions;
(c) each typical occupier, including the actual occupier and owner, is a possible hypothetical tenant;
(d) the tenancy is for one year certain, with a reasonable prospect of continuance;
(e) ability to pay is irrelevant, unless demand is restricted and only one hypothetical tenant exists;
(f) 'tenant's rates and taxes' include only the general rate;
(g) repairs and insurance (under gross value, these are the landlord's responsibility: under net annual value, the tenant's) include internal decoration and cost of putting into good repair;
(h) other expenses necessary to maintain the hereditament in a state to command that rent are limited to expenses in respect of the hereditament itself and those necessary for the continued existence of the hereditament.

7.64 As from the next revaluation (which is due to take effect on 1 April 1990) only 'domestic hereditaments' will be valued to gross value. All other hereditaments will be valued to net annual value direct.

Chapter 8

Principles of assessment

Synopsis

8.1 Having determined whether a hereditament is to be valued to gross or net annual value (see Chapter 7), there are certain principles to bear in mind when fixing that value.

8.2 There are principles which relate only to particular types of property (see Chapter 10), but this chapter will deal with principles which are of general application for most types of hereditaments, some of which may seem obvious as they follow logically from the statutory definitions.

Process of assessment

8.3 The process of arriving at an annual value was described by Lord Denning MR in *R* v *Paddington (VO) ex parte Peachey Property Corporation Ltd* (1965) as follows:

> The rent prescribed by the statute is a *hypothetical* rent, as hypothetical as the tenant. It is the rent which an imaginary tenant might be reasonably expected to pay to an imaginary landlord for a tenancy of this dwelling in this locality, on the hypothesis that both are reasonable people, the landlord not being extortionate, the tenant not being under pressure, the dwelling being vacant and to let, not subject to any control, the landlord agreeing to do the repairs and pay the insurance, the tenant agreeing to pay the rates, the period not too short nor yet too long, simply from year to year.

8.4 Having decided whether a gross value or net annual value is to be calculated for any particular hereditament, the following principles should be considered, where applicable, to assess the correct value for the hereditament.

Individual assessment

8.5   As with any valuation, each property must be valued separately and independently from any others.

8.6   This may seem obvious but, following a case where all the hereditaments in a valuation list were increased by 25 per cent uniformly, it was held that the list was bad because not all hereditaments had been valued individually (*Stirk & Sons Ltd* v *Halifax Assessment Committee* (1922)).

8.7   Similarly, if a non-statutory formula is used to value a hereditament, it will not be relied on in court without an individual valuation of that hereditament (*Dawkins (VO)* v *Royal Leamington Spa Corporation and Warwickshire County Council* (1961)).

Vacant and to let

8.8   In order to consider the rent a tenant would pay for a property, that property must be vacant and available for renting.

8.9   In rating, when a hereditament is (generally) only likely to be valued when it is occupied, it is necessary to fix a rent *assuming* that the property is vacant and available for renting.

8.10   Of course, this is unlikely to be true in fact. Nevertheless, in order to fix a rent under the definitions of gross and net annual value, an assumption of 'vacant and to let' is essential, and follows logically from the assumption of a hypothetical tenancy (see 7.35). After all, even a hypothetical tenant would not pay any rent for a property which is fully occupied.

8.11   In *LCC* v *Erith and West Ham* (1893) Lord Herschell said: 'Whether the premises are in the occupation of the owner or not, the question to be answered is: Supposing they were vacant and to let, what rent might reasonably be expected to be obtained for them?'

Statutory and lease restrictions

8.12   If the hereditament is assumed to be vacant and available for letting on the statutory terms, it follows that *restrictive covenants* and other private arrangements affecting the actual tenancy of the hereditament are irrelevant when ascertaining its value for rating purposes. Under a hypothetical tenancy, a landlord and tenant would conform to the gross or net annual value definitions for their lease.

8.13 On the other hand, every potential hypothetical tenant must be influenced by *statutory restrictions* which affect a hereditament regardless of its actual leasing arrangements (*Port of London Authority* v *Orsett Union* (1920)).

8.14 An exception to this rule is that statutory restrictions *affecting rents paid* for a hereditament are ignored, as a result of the decision of the House of Lords in *Poplar Assessment Committee* v *Roberts* (1922), in which it was held that the annual rent which a hypothetical tenant might reasonably be expected to pay for a hereditament may be something more than can be legally demanded from a tenant under a public general Act.

8.15 It has been held, for example (*O'Mere* v *Burley (VO)* (1968)), that a 'fair rent' determined by the rent officer under the Rent Act 1968 has no direct bearing on the value of a hereditament for rating purposes, because the statutory definition of a 'fair rent' does not correspond to the statutory definition of net annual value.

Rebus sic stantibus

8.16 The property is to be valued *rebus sic stantibus*, ie *things as they stand*. It is not possible to value the property in any physical state other than the one it is in (but see 8.29). It is not possible, for example, to value a house and garage if the garage is not yet constructed, even if planning permission has been granted and a builder engaged.

8.17 It must always be 'the actual house or other property for the occupation of which the occupier is to be rated and that hereditament is to be valued as it in fact is—*rebus sic stantibus* (*Robinson Bros (Brewers) Ltd* v *Houghton and Chester-le-Street Assessment Committee* (1937)).

8.18 The property must be valued as it exists at the date of valuation (see 8.46), ie *rebus sic stantibus*, and not as it once was, or as it might become in the future.

8.19 The principle of *rebus sic stantibus* is considered particularly in relation to three aspects of the property: mode of use, structural alterations, and state of repair.

8.20 In relation to *mode of use*, the property should normally be valued for the use to which it is actually put at the date of the proposal. 'A dwellinghouse must be assessed as a dwellinghouse; a shop as a shop, but not as any particular kind of shop; a factory as a factory, but not as any particular kind of factory'—although any rateable plant and machinery will often limit the use of a factory to one particular user (*Fir Mill Ltd* v *Royton UDC and Jones (VO)* (1960)).

8.21 Although the property has to be valued vacant and to let (see 8.8), it is a generally held principle of rating that the assessment is to be on the basis of the mode or category of occupation of the actual occupier.

8.22 There is, however, no definition of 'mode of use' or 'category of occupation'.

8.23 In *London Transport Executive* v *Croydon LBC and Phillips (VO)* (1974) the tribunal, in rejecting the valuations of a bus garage as a warehouse or a transport depot (all within the same use class), said that another mode of use can only be considered where no beneficial use is being made of the property.

8.24 However, as a result of *Midland Bank Ltd* v *Lanham (VO)* (1978), the Lands Tribunal held that the rental bids of potential tenants in the market, for alternative uses within the same mode or category of use, could be taken into account.

8.25 The tribunal also held that all alternative uses to which the hereditament could actually be put in the real world, and which would be sought after by (hypothetical) tenants in the market, were to be taken as being within the same mode or category of use.

8.26 It is, however, necessary to establish evidence of competition for such uses. Thus, a house can be valued as a house or as a shop or office if there is evidence of demand for those alternative uses, and if planning permission is available for such a change without structural alterations. (See *Henriques* v *Garland (VO)* (1978) where evidence of a lack of demand for a shop, actually used as a dwelling, caused it to be assessed as a dwelling.)

8.27 No *structural alterations* may be envisaged when valuing a hereditament, and while premises are undergoing alteration they must be valued in the state of change in which they are. But the making of a minor alteration of a non-structural nature, provided that it is not so substantial as to change the mode or category of user, may be allowed.

8.28 Thus, when the doors of a domestic garage had been closed with wooden battens so that the building was usable only as a shed, it was held that the removal of those battens was an alteration of a non-structural nature which could be taken into account in the valuation, and so the building was correctly assessed as a garage (*Re Appeal of Sheppard (VO)* (1967)).

8.29 The *state of repair* is an *exception* to the *rebus sic stantibus* rule, because of the repair liability expressed in the statutory definitions of both gross and net annual value. Since both definitions require that repairs be carried out by one of the hypothetical parties to the tenancy, a standard of repair commensurate with the type of property *is to be assumed*, regardless of its actual state of repair.

8.30   It has been held that under the definition of gross value ordinary lack of repair is to be disregarded. It must be assumed that the landlord has carried out his responsibility and that the property is in a reasonable state of repair. (*Causer* v *Thomas (VO)* (1957).)

8.31   In *Anstruther-Gough-Calthorpe* v *McOscar sub nom Calthorpe* v *McOscar* (1923) the **standard of maintenance** was defined as:

> . . . such condition as I should have expected to find them [the premises] in had they been managed by a reasonably minded owner, having full regard to the age of the buildings, the locality, the class of the tenant likely to occupy them, and the maintenance of the property in such a way that only an average amount of annual repair would be necessary in the future.

8.32   It has been held that poor decorative repair, cracks in the ceilings and walls, resetting of window frames, damp in the kitchen ceiling and wall, a defective hot-water tank, and the stove out of order, were considered to be reasonable repairs for a landlord to carry out, and that the rent agreed would be based on the assumption that the repairs had been carried out (*Wexler* v *Playle (VO)* (1960)).

8.33   However, although ordinary lack of repair may not be taken into account, **serious lack of repair or defects**, particularly structural ones, may be taken into account in certain circumstances, where it would be unreasonable or impossible for a landlord to repair.

8.34   In *Saunders* v *Malby (VO)* (1976) the Court of Appeal held that the principle in *Wexler* v *Playle* does not mean that disrepair capable of remedy must always be disregarded. Only disrepair which the hypothetical landlord might reasonably be expected to remedy, rather than accept a reduced rent, may be ignored. This involves considering not only the extent and the nature of the disrepair and whether it was capable of remedy, but also whether it would be economical for the hypothetical landlord to carry out such repairs.

8.35   In valuing direct to net annual value, where the tenant is responsible for repairs etc the same principles should be applied.

Tenant fresh on the scene

8.36   The hypothetical tenant has been described '. . . as a reasonably minded person, arriving fresh on the scene without any prejudice which might derive from experience of conditions which obtained previously' (*Finnis* v *Priest (VO)* (1959)).

8.37   Thus, it is not possible to compare previous conditions with those prevailing at the date of valuation.

8.38   What must be determined is the effect on the mind of the 'reasonably minded person' who has no previous knowledge of the property or locality, of conditions at the date of valuation, and how those conditions will affect his rental bid.

Consider all relevant evidence

8.39   As with valuations for any other purpose, all factors which affect the rental value of property (other than those which rating law specifically ignores) must be taken into account in assessing gross or net annual value.

8.40   Consideration can thus be given to the economic effects of war (*Staley* v *Castleton Overseers* (1864)), a strike, credit restrictions, development plans or any other phenomenon which affects rent paid.

8.41   In *Beath* v *Poole (VO)* (1973) the Lands Tribunal reduced the assessment of a house affected by the construction of a motorway due to be completed well over a year after the date of the proposal (see 9.48).

8.42   Net annual value is the rent which a tenant might reasonably be expected to pay and, in estimating this rent, all that could reasonably affect the mind of the intending tenant ought to be considered (*Cartwright* v *Sculcoates Union* (1899)).

8.43   However, the annual rent is fixed as at the date of the proposal, and it is the effect of actual disabilities on the mind of the hypothetical tenant as at that date which is to be considered (*Nightingale (VO)* v *Harrap* (1970)).

8.44   The degree of certainty with which future events can be predicted will vary with those events. This does not make the influence of the events irrelevant to the rental bid. It means only that the weight given to the effects of future events must be carefully considered (*Robinson Bros (Brewers) Ltd* v *Houghton and Chester-le-Street Assessment Committee* (1937)).

8.45   In *Garton* v *Hunter (VO)* (1968) the court held that valuations based on all methods of valuation were allowed; the 'goodness or badness' of the evidence went to its weighting, not its admissibility.

Valuation date

8.46 As with all valuations, it is essential to have a date at which to value the property. However, in rating this may be a complicated issue.

8.47 In *Barratt* v *Gravesend Assessment Committee* (1941) it was held that it was necessary to determine what annual rent a hypothetical tenant would pay as at *the date of the proposal* for the alteration of the valuation list. Thus, once a valuation list has come into force, the valuation date is the date of the proposal to alter that list. In *Ladies' Hosiery & Underwear Ltd* v *West Middlesex Assessment Committee* (1932) the appellant company proved that its rating assessment was too high in comparison with the assessments of seven similar properties in the locality, but accepted that the assessment was not in excess of the rent that might reasonably be expected for its property on the statutory terms at the date of the proposal. The Court of Appeal rejected the contention that the assessment should be reduced to the same level as the seven comparable hereditaments, because the assessment was correct. Thus, in *Ladies' Hosiery* it was held that *correctness of assessment must not be sacrificed to uniformity of assessment*.

8.48 Prior to the time when the case was decided, fairness and uniformity had been recognised as a consideration in valuation for rating.

8.49 A series of case decisions resulted in the basic principle that correctness of valuation must not be sacrificed to uniformity, and that any *unfairness must be remedied by achieving uniform correctness* and not by creating uniform incorrectness.

8.50 This problem does not exist on the creation of a new valuation list, because in such circumstances all hereditaments are valued as at the same date, ie the date when the list takes effect. The problem only arises during the life of a valuation list and is aggravated by inflation and disproportionate increases in rental values for different properties in the same locality.

8.51 Because the *Ladies' Hosiery* rule that correctness must not be sacrificed to uniformity was strictly followed, and because revaluations were infrequent (1939, 1956, 1963, 1973), the situation became very difficult.

8.52 There was a level of values established by the then existing valuation list, say 1939, and since the war values had increased. So that if a person, say in 1950, proposed an alteration to an assessment, the valuation date was 1950, under the *Barratt* v *Gravesend* rule. However, if a 1950 rental value were correctly adopted for this property, any other similar property would still remain assessed at the original 1939 values, assuming there had been no alteration to those assessments. Because correctness of assessment must not be sacrificed to uniformity, the only remedy an occupier had was to make proposals on all other comparable hereditaments to have their values increased to the 1950 level.

8.53 The Lands Tribunal attempted to tackle this situation by calling the then current rental value 'a rent paid in extreme scarcity by persons in dire necessity' (*Thomas* v *Cross* (1951)) and by giving increased weight to the evidence of comparable assessments, so that the general level of value, or *tone*, could be maintained within the life of a valuation list.

8.54 By s 17 of the Local Government Act 1966, now s 20 GRA 1967, statutory 'tone of the list' was introduced. It applies to the ascertainment of a value or altered value of a hereditament as the result of a proposal for the alteration of the valuation list (ie not when the list first takes effect).

8.55 The effect of the section is that the hereditament, its locality and matters affecting the amenities of the locality, are taken to be in their state at the date of the proposal, but the value ascribed to the hereditament is that which would have been ascribed to it had it been in existence during the year before the valuation list came into force, ie its *value* according to the *tone of the list*.

What the statute actually says is:

> For the purposes of any alterations of a valuation list to be made . . . in pursuance of a proposal, the value or altered value to be ascribed to the hereditament under s 19 of this Act *shall not exceed* the value which would have been ascribed thereto in that list if the hereditament had been subsisting throughout the year before that in which the valuation list came into force . . .

8.56 Section 20, therefore, creates a *ceiling value*, which is the level of values as at the date when the list came into force.

8.57 Thus, a new house assessed today to be worth an annual rental value on the statutory terms of £1,200 per annum, must be assessed at £500 per annum if that is the value which would have been ascribed to it had it been in existence the year before the 1973 list came into force—values being as at 1973, conditions as they prevail today.

8.58 Because s 20 creates a ceiling value, if it can be shown that today's rental value on the statutory terms is less than the tone of the list rental value, then the *Barratt* v *Gravesend* rule applies, and the value as at the date of the proposal can be allowed.

8.59 It is, therefore, necessary to carry out two valuations of each hereditament, one as at the date of the proposal (s 19) and one on 'tone of the list' (s 20). It is the lower value which should be adopted.

8.60 What s 20 goes on to state is that:

. . . the value . . . shall not exceed the value which would have been ascribed . . . if the hereditament had been subsisting throughout the relevant year . . . [ie the year before that in which the valuation list came into force]; . . . on the assumptions that . . .

(a) the hereditament was in the same *state* as at the time of valuation and any *relevant factors* . . . were those subsisting at the last mentioned time; and

(b) the locality in which the hereditament is situated was in the same state, so far as concerns the other premises situated in that locality and the occupation and age of those premises, the transport services and other facilities available and other matters affecting the amenities of the locality . . .

8.61 The expression *relevant factors* means:

(a) the mode or category of occupation of the hereditament;
(b) the quantity of minerals in or extracted from the hereditament;
(c) the volume of trade or business carried on in the case of a public house.

8.62 When dealing with properties valued on the profits basis (see 9.51–69), it is necessary to adopt the accounts which would have been available during the relevant year, still considering the physical property as at the date of the proposal.

8.63 Following the decisions in *Addis Ltd* v *Clement (VO)* (1987), *Sheerness Steel Co plc* v *Maudling (VO)* (1986) and *Thorn EMI Cinemas Ltd* v *Harrison (VO)* (1986), there is a clearer definition of the assumption that 'the hereditament was in the same *state* as at the time of valuation . . .', ie date of the proposal.

8.64 In *Addis* the Court of Appeal accepted that 'in general . . . s 20(1)(*b*) is limited to physical factors or factors which affect the physical enjoyment of a hereditament'. Thus for valuation purposes '. . . it is the economic climate, both local and national, of 1973 which has to be considered and not that at the date of the proposal except to the extent that alterations in the economic conditions result in changes in the locality which are capable of being observed "on the ground" in the locality'.

8.65 In *Thorn EMI Cinemas* the decrease in the volume of trade, as reflected in the number of admissions, resulted in a reduction in the assessment of the cinema.

The value of most if not all premises which are used for commercial purposes, and this applies most clearly in the case of retail shops, must depend in a broad sense upon the volume of trade or business carried on, and in arriving at the notional value of such premises on the artificial assumptions to be found in s 20 *it is quite impossible to exclude the element of value attributable to the volume of trade or business*.

8.66 Following the House of Lords decision in *K Shoe Shops Ltd* v *Hardy (VO)* (1983), it was held that the correct date of valuation on a revaluation is the date the valuation list came into force, ie for the present valuation list 1 April 1973.

8.67 However, with the introduction of s 19A into GRA 1967 (introduced by LGPLA 1980, s 30), ie with the Secretary of State for the Environment now able to specify a valuation date for any future valuation list (an antecedent valuation date), no further difficulties should arise on a revaluation.

Checklist

8.68 Each hereditament must be independently assessed.

8.69 The hereditament is valued vacant and to let.

8.70 Private arrangements and restrictive covenants are ignored. Only statutory restrictions which do not relate to the level of rent paid can be taken into account.

8.71 The property is to be valued *rebus sic stantibus*, ie as it stands. Consider:

    (a) mode of occupation;
    (b) structural alterations;
    (c) state of repair—this is the exception, so assume an adequate state of repair.

8.72 Tenant is assumed to be 'fresh on the scene'.

8.73 Consider all the relevant evidence which affects the value of the property.

8.74 The valuation date is the date of the proposal bearing in mind tone of the list. Because correctness of the assessment must not be sacrificed to uniformity, to achieve uniform correctness the level of value established by a valuation list is retained throughout the life of that list—tone of the list—s 20. Section 20 creates a ceiling value above which a (normal) valuation cannot go.

8.75 Consider as at the date of the proposal the hereditament, locality, amenities affecting the locality, mode of occupation, quantity of minerals, volume of trade passing in a public house, the legal and the economic state of the hereditament etc. Consider as at the 'relevant year' (ie the year before that in which the list came into force) levels of value.

8.76 On a revaluation, the list must be correct as at the date the list takes effect. On a future revaluation, the Secretary of State may specify an earlier date for all valuations.

Chapter 9

Methods of valuation

Synopsis

9.1 With one major exception, any of the traditional methods of valuation are acceptable in assessing gross or net annual value.

9.2 The one exception is the statutory requirement that certain hereditaments be valued according to a formula laid down by statute.

9.3 Assessment by statutory formula is required for almost all premises occupied by statutory undertakings, eg gas and electricity boards, and certain other public bodies.

9.4 It is, therefore, essential to eliminate statutory formulae as a means of arriving at net annual value, before considering the most appropriate method of valuation to be adopted.

9.5 The use of rental evidence, profits method and the contractor's test are all acceptable ways of calculating gross or net annual value, provided they are adapted to conform with the statutory definitions.

9.6 It is accepted that evidence from more than one method of valuation may be used. Although one method may be more appropriate than another, this does not mean that other evidence should be ignored. It merely means that more reliance will be placed on the most suitable method.

9.7 It is not uncommon for the rating assessments of comparable properties to be used to support other valuation evidence. In the case of such properties as dwellinghouses, assessments of comparable hereditaments may be the only evidence available on which an assessment can be made.

Choice of valuation method

9.8 With the exception of the need for a statutory formula, *there is no legal requirement to use any particular method* of arriving at a gross or net annual value.

9.9 In fact, in the past courts have accepted 'spot valuations', provided by experienced and qualified valuers, without any supporting evidence (see eg *Ryde on Rating*, p 464).

9.10 In *Port of London Authority* v *Orsett Union* (1920) Lord Dunedin made it plain that *it is the nature and circumstances of the property which will dictate the method of valuation adopted*, and that 'no question of law is necessarily involved'.

9.11 In *Garton* v *Hunter (VO)* (1968) the court held that valuations produced by all methods of valuation *are admissible as evidence. The 'goodness or badness' of the evidence* went to its weighting, not its admissibility:

> Where the particular hereditament is let on what is plainly a rack rent and there are similar hereditaments and similar economic sites which are so let that they are truly comparable, that evidence should be classified in respect of cogency as a category of admissible evidence properly described as superior; in some, but not all, cases, that category may be exclusive. Any indirect evidence, albeit relevant, should be placed in a different category; reference to the latter category may or may not be proper, or indeed necessary, according to the degree of weight of the former kind of evidence.

9.12 And later, in effectively stating that *all methods of valuation should produce the same answer*, the court said:

> . . . we do not look upon any of these tests as being either a 'right' method or a 'wrong' method of valuation; all three are means to the same end; all three are legitimate ways of seeking to arrive at a rental figure that would correspond with an actual market rent on the statutory hypothesis and if they are properly applied all the tests should in fact point to the same answer; but the greater the margin for error in any particular test, the less is the weight that can be attached to it.

Assessment by statutory formula

9.13 Originally, property occupied by statutory undertakings was valued on the profits basis. In more recent years such undertakers are not required to make a profit and, therefore, the use of the profits basis ceased to be appropriate.

9.14 In ss 30–34, as amended by s 19 of the Local Government Act 1974, a series of statutory formulae is laid down for application to certain premises occupied by the following:

(a) statutory water undertakers, but *not dwellings*, in their occupation;

(b) railway and canal premises occupied by a transport board, but *not dwellings, hotels etc, or office premises* in their occupation (like the Crown, transport boards make contributions in lieu of rates);

(c) electricity and gas boards, but *not any dwellings, or shops* used for sale etc of appliances;

(d) British Coal, but *not in respect of offices* not involved in the administration of a mine, *and research premises*;

(e) The Post Office is *only exempt* in respect of kiosks, posts, wires etc, and its underground railway;

(f) docks and harbour undertakings.

9.15 In addition to the above, The Secretary of State has power to prescribe formulae for:

(a) county and voluntary school premises;

(b) hereditaments occupied by an undertaking for the diffusion by wire of sound or television programmes.

No orders have yet been made in relation to these.

9.16 The Secretary of State has power to amend any of the provisions relating to statutory formulae, subject to parliamentary approval.

9.17 Thus, having ascertained that a statutory formula is not applicable in valuing a particular hereditament, any of the traditional methods of valuation may be adopted to produce a net annual value, provided that it conforms to the requirements of the statutory definitions of gross or net annual value.

Rental evidence

9.18 Because it is necessary to arrive at a gross or net annual value, a rental value under the terms of the hypothetical tenancy has to be found (see 7.29–47). It is, therefore, obvious that the best evidence for finding a rental value should be rental evidence.

9.19 Rental evidence, where available, should always be investigated to see whether it can be relied on to produce a gross or net annual value, even if evidence produced by other methods seems appropriate (*Garton* v *Hunter (VO)* (1968)—see 9.11–12).

9.20 Both direct and indirect rental evidence should be investigated. ('Direct' rental evidence is the rent passing on the hereditament to be valued: 'indirect' rental evidence is the rent passing on comparable hereditaments.)

9.21 Although the actual occupier must be regarded as a possible hypothetical tenant, the rent an actual occupier pays is not automatically the gross or net annual value.

9.22 However, in the absence of evidence to the contrary, the rent actually passing on the hereditament may be considered as a basis for gross or net annual value.

9.23 The rent passing must, therefore, be tested to ensure that it conforms to the statutory definition of gross or net annual value, before it can be used as evidence.

9.24 A rent passing will not be a basis for gross or net annual value if it includes other property, such as goodwill, if there are onerous covenants, or where there was some other reason to suggest that the rent paid was a misconception and that were the lease to be renegotiated, a different rent would be paid (*East London Railway Joint Committee* v *Greenwich Union* (1890)).

9.25 Some actual rents can be eliminated as a result of case law decisions. Thus, controlled rents and 'fair' rents are both useless for rating purposes (see 8.14–15) (*Poplar Assessment Committee* v *Roberts* (1922) and *O'Mere* v *Burley (VO)* (1968)). Rents fixed by tender are of little or no value as evidence (*Leisure UK Ltd* v *Moore (VO)* (1975)) as are council house rents (*LCC* v *Wand (VO)* (1957)).

Adjustments

9.26 Few rents are paid on terms which exactly match the statutory definitions of gross or net annual value. It is, therefore, necessary to adjust actual rents so that they conform to the statutory definitions.

9.27 This will involve, for example, deducting **rates** where they are included in the rent passing to the landlord, since in both definitions rates are paid by the tenant.

9.28 ***Capital payments made in accordance with the lease*** are assumed to have reduced the rent negotiated. Such payments are therefore treated as capitalised rent.

9.29 Such capital payments must be reduced to an annual equivalent and added to the rent to find full rental value when the rent was fixed.

9.30 In calculating an annual equivalent, dual-rate, untaxed years' purchase figures are used (*FW Woolworth & Co Ltd* v *Peck (VO)* (1967)) for the term for which the rent is reduced, ie the full term of the lease or the period until the next rent review which requires full rental value to be paid.

9.31 The tenant has paid a reduced rent because the capital expenditure was made. However, the capital payment may reflect a reduced rent over a shorter or longer period than the term of the lease. Thus, a lease for twenty-one years with the payment of a premium may allow for a rent review to full rental value after three, seven or fourteen years, or not at all. Such capital expenditure must always be considered in the light of the terms of the actual lease and, if there is a real prospect of rent remaining reduced for a longer period than the term of the lease, the capital expenditure should be amortised over that longer period (*Edma (Jewellers) Ltd* v *Moore (VO)* (1975)).

9.32 If a *reverse premium* is paid, the annual equivalent of that premium is deducted from the rent passing. (A 'reverse premium' is a capital sum paid to an incoming tenant to encourage him to take a lease, or paid to a landlord to encourage him to accept the surrender of a lease. This will occur, for example, when the rent passing under lease exceeds the rental value of the property.)

9.33 *Capital payments not paid in accordance with the lease* are not considered to have resulted in a reduced rent. It is, therefore, necessary to establish whether the capital payments have increased the rental value of the premises.

9.34 If such capital payments have increased the rental value of the premises, that increased rental value can be established more reliably by using rental evidence from comparable improved properties, rather than the annual equivalent of the capital payments.

9.35 Both gross and net annual value specify liability for *repairs, insurance* and *other expenses*. It is, therefore, necessary to ensure that, when calculating a gross value, the landlord is responsible for these outgoings and, when calculating a net annual value, the tenant is responsible for them.

9.36 In both cases, repairs include internal decorations and the cost of putting the hereditament in good order, if that is necessary (*Wexler* v *Playle (VO)* (1960)).

9.37 It is not usual for valuers to deduct actual costs for repairs, insurance etc, and the courts have accepted a 'rule of thumb' deduction of ten per cent of full rental value to reflect all outgoings (five per cent external and five per cent internal repairs), eg *Trevail (VO)* v *C & A Modes Ltd* (1967).

9.38 As with all rules of thumb, their use creates anomalies, but the courts seem likely to accept the ten per cent rule for all usual hereditaments unless there are exceptional circumstances.

9.39 Where rent paid includes an amount to cover *landlord's services*, a deduction must be made from the rent to cover the services.

9.40 Under s 23, where rent paid includes provision for *landlord's services* to premises not comprising the hereditament, and where a rental method is being used to calculate a gross value, only the cost of certain services can be deducted from the rent paid.

9.41 In making deductions from gross rent in such circumstances, no deduction is made for repairs, maintenance and insurance to the common parts, landlord's profit on services or the cost of rent collection (see Chapter 10).

9.42 Where s 23 does not apply (see 9.40), the cost of all landlord's services is deductible (*Bell Property Trust Ltd* v *Hampstead Assessment Committee* (1940)).

9.43 For both definitions, a rent must be fixed *from year to year*. Thus, annual rents are the best evidence; however, such rents are rare.

9.44 The courts have accepted that rents fixed for longer terms *can* equate to annual rents if the lease is for a relatively short period or if the lease has rent review provisions at suitable intervals.

9.45 The courts do, however, require that such rents are tested to ensure that they conform to an annual rent.

Analysis

9.46 Having selected and adjusted rents, it is necessary to analyse them into a *unit of comparison*, so that the rental value of one hereditament can be compared to that of another similar hereditament.

9.47 The unit of comparison will vary with type of property involved, eg shops are compared using a price per square metre in terms of 'zone A'.

9.48 However, the unit price will reflect only those factors which affect the value of the properties analysed. If the property to be valued suffers from *disadvantages or disabilities* not found in the analysed properties, an end allowance must be made to reflect these factors.

9.49 Only those disadvantages and disabilities not reflected in the unit price which affect the rental bid of the hypothetical tenant must be taken into account.

9.50 Nuisances which affect ownership, a particular (rather than a hypothetical) occupier or are typical for the type of property in its locality must be ignored.

The profits method

9.51 The profits method is a method of valuation used for property which is seldom let, and where there is often an element of factual or legal monopoly. (A factual monopoly arises where the position of the premises is unique and the business could only be carried on in that place, or where there are no other suitable sites. A legal monopoly exists where a licence is required to operate the business or where statute grants a monopoly.)

9.52 Although profits are not rateable, the ability to earn profits may affect the rent and, in the absence of more direct evidence, offer some guide as to rental value. If the object of the tenant most likely to rent the premises is to make a profit, the amount of that profit is likely to influence the rent which the tenant will be prepared to give.

9.53 It is the facility to make trade profits afforded by a particular hereditament to the hypothetical tenant which must be found, and not necessarily the profits made by a particular trader.

9.54 If premises are occupied for profit, '*any restrictions which the law has imposed* upon the profit-earning capacity of the undertaking must of course be considered' in estimating the rateable value (*LCC* v *Erith and West Ham* (1893)).

9.55 Statute can limit profits in two ways:

    (a) by limiting the prices which a trader can charge; and
    (b) by appropriating the whole or part of any profits to particular objectives, eg taxation.

9.56 Case law shows that limitations described in (a) above must be taken into account, but limitations described in (b) must not.

9.57 It is recognised that the hypothetical tenant must occupy under the same statutory restrictions as the actual tenant.

9.58 Where property occupied by a local authority is valued using the profits method, it may be necessary to increase the rent produced by the profits method to take into account the local authority's *overbid*, ie the additional motives which a local authority as a hypothetical tenant may have over and above those of a purely commercial competitor (*Taunton Borough Council* v *Sture (VO)* (1958); *Lowestoft Borough Council* v *Scaife (VO)* (1960)).

9.59 The principle of 'overbid' can be criticised since the amount of overbid is necessarily an arbitrary figure which is not capable of being quantified with market evidence.

9.60 Where possible, it is usual to take three years' *accounts*, and to average their amounts in order to arrive at figures to be used for valuation.

9.61 The *accounts* to be considered are those last published, or available to the hypothetical tenant, at *the date of the proposal*, in three cases:

(a) hereditaments occupied by a public utility undertaking and valued on the profits basis;

(b) public houses, where the volume of trade or business is to be regarded as that subsisting at the date of the proposal;

(c) hereditaments valued on the profits basis where the volume of trade (and hence the value) has reduced since the original valuation date. (This arises from the general provisions of s 20 that no assessment shall exceed the tone value.)

9.62 However, in other cases the valuation is to be on the *tone of the list*, and the relevant accounts used are the latest ones available to the valuation officer when he prepared the valuation list.

9.63 The practice has been to base the valuation on the last accounts available prior to the date of valuation, but to admit in evidence the latest available accounts to the date of the proposal where these illustrate the working of factors in existence at the date of valuation. Where the latest accounts show the workings of a factor which would not have influenced the mind of the hypothetical tenant at the date of valuation, they are inadmissible as evidence.

9.64 From the decision in *Kingston Union* v *Metropolitan Water Board* (1926), the *profits basis* may be summarised as shown below.

9.65 From the gross receipts of the undertaking deduct working expenses, an allowance for tenant's profit and the cost of repairs and other deductions, and treat the balance remaining as the rateable value and rates. In outline, the valuation is as follows:

(a) *adjusted gross receipts*: gross receipts (adjusted if necessary to show only those receipts relating to the running of the undertaking)

   less

(b) *adjusted working expenses*: working expenses (adjusted to exclude rent and rates: if NAV is to be calculated direct, include repairs and insurance of the hereditament; if GV is to be calculated, exclude these)
equals *divisible balance*
less
(c) *tenant's share*: comprising,
   (i) interest on capital invested, including cash in bank, fixtures and fittings, stock, contingency fund etc;
   (ii) risk;
   (iii) remuneration.
Tenant's share is usually taken as a percentage of either gross receipts, tenant's capital or divisible balance
equals *rent and rates*.

Adjusted gross receipts less *adjusted working expenses* equals *divisible balance* less *tenant's share* equals *rent and rates*.

9.66 Gross receipts and working expenses are ascertained from the actual accounts. It is important to remember that the rent to be ascertained is *the rent which the hypothetical tenant will pay* on the statutory terms, not necessarily the rent which the actual occupier would pay.

9.67 The hypothetical tenant is a businessman of average competence. If the actual occupier is above or below average competence, his accounts will need to be adjusted before they can be used in the valuation.

9.68 In assessing the proper share for the tenant, it is important to allow return on capital invested, as well as an amount to cover risk and remuneration in running the business. These three items must be included and a percentage of either gross receipts, tenant's capital or divisible balance, taken to cover them. In all three cases, whichever one is chosen, the higher the risk, the higher the percentage that the tenant will require.

9.69 In valuing on the profits basis, remember also that s 21 of the GRA 1967 excludes valuations on the profits basis from its provisions. All *plant and machinery* in a hereditament is, therefore, rateable.

The contractor's test

9.70 Where property is of a type which is rarely let, interest on the capital value or on the actual cost of land and buildings may be used as a guide to ascertaining rental value.

9.71 The net annual value is defined by statute as the rent which might reasonably be expected. Interest on cost or on capital value cannot replace net annual value but, in the absence of other evidence, it can be looked at as prima facie evidence in order to answer the question of what rent a tenant might reasonably be expected to pay.

9.72 There is authority from court decisions to support this practice. In fact, even where rental evidence is available, interest on cost or capital value is admissible, although consideration must be given to its weighting as evidence.

9.73 In *R* v *School Board for London* (1885) Cave J said:

> Interest on cost is a rough test undoubtedly. It is a test in some cases but not a test in others. If the place is occupied by a tenant, it is not a good test at all, because the rent which he actually pays is a far better one . . . But if the place is occupied by the owner himself, then it is in some sense a test, a rough test no doubt, and only prima facie evidence, but still some evidence, to show what the value of the occupation is. . . . if he could get the place cheaper, at a less rent than the interest on the cost comes to, it is to be assumed he would not go to the expense of building, he would prefer to take the cheaper course and pay the rent.

9.74 Although, as a result of *Garton* v *Hunter (VO)* (1968), cost or capital value can be referred to even where rental evidence is available, it is rare that it will be preferred to actual rents, or to evidence based on the profits method or to assessments of comparable hereditaments. The contractor's test tends to be a method of last resort.

9.75 The Lands Tribunal has frequently rejected the contractor's test in favour of one of the other methods of valuation currently used in rating.

9.76 In *Cardiff Rating Authority and Cardiff Assessment Committee* v *Guest Keen Baldwin's Iron and Steel Co Ltd* (1949), Denning LJ said:

> Even when the contractor's basis is taken, the assessment on that basis is open to great variations up and down, as, for instance, in assessing the effective capital value and in deciding what percentage to take on it . . . The possible variations may become so great that the contractor's basis ceases to be a significant factor in the assessment. In such a situation the tribunal of fact may prefer to take some other basis. . .

9.77 The contractor's test may also be useless as a guide to annual value if the evidence shows that the hypothetical tenant would not have paid a rent based on cost.

9.78 Nevertheless, it is a recognised method of calculating gross and net annual value, even though it is probably the least reliable.

9.79 What has to be determined is not what the landlord would ask, but *what a tenant would give*. The landlord is assumed to be a person willing to let to a tenant willing to take, neither being in a position to dictate terms (*R* v *Paddington (VO) ex parte Peachey Property Corporation Ltd* (1965)), so that consideration of the landlord's costs is wrong. However, reference to cost of capital value can be justified from a tenant's point of view.

9.80 In *Cardiff City Council* v *Williams (VO)* (1973) Lord Denning MR described the following passage (from the Solicitor General in *Dawkins (VO)* v *Royal Leamington Spa Corporation and Warwickshire County Council* (1961)) as the 'classic explanation' of the contractor's basis:

> As I understand it, the argument is that the hypothetical tenant has an *alternative to leasing* the hereditament and paying rent for it; *he can build* a precisely similar building himself. He could borrow the money, on which he would have to pay interest; or use his own capital on which he would have to forgo interest to put up a similar building for his owner-occupation rather than rent it, and he will do that rather than pay what he would regard as an excessive rent—that is, a rent which is greater than the interest he forgoes by using his own capital to build the building himself. The argument is that he will therefore be unwilling to pay more as an annual rent for a hereditament than it would cost him in the way of annual interest on the capital sum necessary to build a similar hereditament. On the other hand, if the annual rent demanded is *fixed marginally below* what it would cost him in the way of annual interest on the capital sum necessary to build a similar hereditament, it will be in his interest to rent the hereditament rather than build it.

9.81 Thus, the contractor's test should produce a *ceiling rent* above which the rent under the statutory definition should not go.

Method of application of contractor's test

9.82 Where cost and value are closely related, as with new buildings, this method of valuation may involve the application of appropriate percentages to the actual cost of construction of the buildings and to the cost of acquiring the land.

9.83   However, with the increase in building costs, a wide gap between cost and value means that a modification to the method is essential if it is to produce credible net annual values.

9.84   Accordingly, after the cost of construction has been calculated, that cost is reduced to one which represents the *effective capital value* of the hereditament, ie the market value of the hereditament in a form effective for its purpose. The appropriate percentage is then applied to the effective capital value (ECV).

9.85   In *Gilmore (VO)* v *Baker-Carr (No 2)* (1963) the Lands Tribunal recognised five stages in applying the contractor's basis (see also table 10.205).

First stage

9.86   Estimate the *cost of construction* of the building. There is a difference of opinion as to whether it is better to take the cost of replacing the actual building as it is, or the cost of a substitute building providing identical accommodation, but in a modern building. The simple substitute building estimate is usually preferred as being the most likely structure to be replaced.

Second stage

9.87   It is very important to distinguish between value and cost. This applies equally, whether the cost is the actual cost of providing the hereditament or the estimated cost of providing a simple substitute building. If a house is built at a cost of £100,000 but could have been constructed for less, the lower figure is the basis upon which the calculation must be based. But there is a distinction between expenditure which is unforeseen and accidental, and expenditure which is deliberately undertaken; the former should be ignored, and the latter taken into account.

9.88   Make *deductions* from the cost of construction to allow for age, obsolescence and any other factors necessary to arrive at the *effective capital value*. In *Imperial College of Science and Technology* v *Ebdon and Westminster City Council* (1984) the Lands Tribunal considered that an 'effective capital value' could be more accurately described as an *'adjusted replacement cost'*. The object of this stage is to adjust the cost of the substitute building to allow for the actual state of the existing building, so that it is not a conversion of cost into value. If there is sufficient evidence of relevant capital transactions, there seems to be no reason, in principle, why the valuation should not begin at this stage.

9.89   In valuing older buildings, deductions, often large in amount, may be necessary in order to take account of age and obsolescence.

The effective capital value (or adjusted replacement cost) has been determined for buildings, some of them built centuries ago, by imagining either a replacement of or a substitute for them and then comparing, in terms of value, the replacement or substitute buildings with the actual buildings. This comparison has usually involved reference to a scale of deductions for age and obsolescence devised and used in the assessment of local authority schools (see paras 10.189–94), applied according to the judgement of the valuer. It is disabilities which affect, for example, the operating efficiency of the hereditament which will reduce costs to effective capital values.

Third stage

9.90 Establish the *cost of the land*. The principle of *rebus sic stantibus* demands that the land be valued as if limited to its existing use. The value of the site may reflect advantages or disadvantages not accounted for in the effective capital value of the substitute building, but properly to be accounted for in the adjusted cost of that building. Thus, deductions made from building costs and land values may be different.

Fourth stage

9.91 *Apply the market rate* or rates at which money can be borrowed or invested to the effective capital value of the buildings and the land. To the 'real rate of interest' allow for the advantages which an owner has and which are not available to an occupier; the ability to pay of the hypothetical tenant, if there is only one likely hypothetical tenant; add for a *borrower's premium* (if appropriate), *inflation, depreciation* and the *repair liability* for gross value (*Imperial College*). Lands Tribunal cases have indicated the following rates as appropriate:
  (a) 3.5 per cent—public schools, University and Oxford and Cambridge colleges;
  (b) 4.5 per cent—non-profit making local authority undertakings;
  (c) 5 per cent—local authority schools and industrial (special) properties to net annual value;
  (d) 6 per cent—commercially run sports facilities and industrial (special) properties to gross value.

9.92 The percentage of effective capital value which is to be taken as annual value will be affected by the motive of the hypothetical tenant in taking the hereditament and his ability to pay. The application of a market rate to the effective capital value may be inappropriate as that would show what it would cost in annual terms to become an owner of the hereditament. Owners have advantages which occupiers do not have (eg a permanent interest in the property, freedom to alter or improve it, the benefit of capital appreciation); an annual tenancy is therefore less valuable than ownership, and the annual rent must be fixed below the interest charge.

9.93 The fact that a particular occupier can borrow money at low rates of interest, or can obtain money in the form of benefactor or government grants, is irrelevant. The motive of the hypothetical tenant in taking the hereditament and his ability to pay for it can be relevant considerations in determining the rate per cent.

Fifth stage

9.94 The object of this stage is to take into account *any items that have not already been considered* in valuing the buildings and land, in order to arrive at the annual equivalent of the likely capital cost to the hypothetical tenant. Such considerations may include poor site access and the inflexibility of a district heating scheme (*Imperial College*).

Sixth stage

9.95 This stage was added by the Lands Tribunal in *Imperial College*. Consider if the result of the fifth stage is likely to be pushed up or down in the negotiations between a hypothetical landlord and a hypothetical tenant, having regard to the relative *bargaining strength* of the parties.

9.96 The Lands Tribunal, while accepting the contractor's basis as 'a poor best', has criticised 'the artificiality of the approach' (*Downing, Newnham, Churchill and Kings Colleges, Cambridge* v *City of Cambridge and Allsop (VO)* (1968)). However, in *Eton College (Provost and Fellows)* v *Lane (VO) and Eton UDC* (1971) the tribunal said:

> Provided a valuer using this approach is sufficiently experienced, and is aware of what he is doing, and knows just how he is using his particular variant of the method, and provided he constantly keeps in mind what he is comparing with what, we are satisfied that the contractor's basis provides a valuation instrument at least as precise as any other approach.

Use of assessments of comparable hereditaments

9.97 Although hardly a method of valuation, reference to assessments of comparable hereditaments is widely used to ascertain gross or net annual value of a hereditament where better evidence is lacking, or in order to supplement other evidence.

9.98 In *Howarth* v *Price (VO)* (1965) the Lands Tribunal said:

> Where however there is a paucity of satisfactory direct rental evidence, then the best evidence as to rental value is likely to be the 'indirect' evidence provided by the gross values of similar hereditaments.

9.99 When basing the assessment of a hereditament on comparable assessments the Lands Tribunal said (in *Lamb* v *Minards (VO)* (1974)): '. . . with the passage of time the volume of established assessments acquires weight as evidence of accepted values . . .', and it seems that at least twelve months must pass after a revaluation in order to establish (and presumably test) a tone of the list for values of hereditaments in any given area before they can be used as evidence on which to base comparable assessments.

9.100 The assessments of comparable hereditaments are admissible as evidence of value and also as an admission of value by the valuation officer. It seems that a valuation officer cannot deny the accuracy of the assessments in his own area, whether made by him or a predecessor.

9.101 However, an assessment under appeal is customarily excluded from consideration as being unlikely to provide reliable evidence of value (*Thomas Scott & Sons (Bakers) Ltd* v *Davies (VO)* (1969)).

9.102 The more unusual the hereditament, the further afield it is possible to go for comparable assessments. For example, in *Shrewsbury Schools* v *Shrewsbury Borough Council and Plumpton (VO)* (1960) the tribunal admitted evidence of the assessments of ninety-nine public schools in all parts of the country. But in the case of ordinary types of hereditaments, such as houses or shops, evidence of assessments outside the locality will usually be of little or no value.

9.103 For all classes of hereditament it is acceptable to refer to assessments throughout the country in order to illustrate *valuation practice and method* (*William Hill (Hove) Ltd* v *Burton (VO)* (1958)).

9.104 Comparable assessments are used extensively for the fixing of gross values for dwellings (see 10.6–22).

Checklist

9.105 Having eliminated the requirement for a statutory formula, evidence produced by all methods of valuation can be used. Some methods will be more or less appropriate to the circumstances, but that will influence their weight as evidence not their admissibility.

9.106   In all cases, the methods of valuation must be based on the *statutory definitions* and the *hypothetical tenancy*.

Rental evidence

9.107   Where available, rents should always be investigated and, if reliable and suitable, *adjusted* to conform to the statutory definition.

9.108   The actual rent is not necessarily the same as that paid by a hypothetical tenant, but in the absence of evidence to the contrary, may be considered as a basis for gross or net annual value.

9.109   Adjusted rents must be analysed to an appropriate unit of comparison.

9.110   End allowances must be made for disadvantages or disabilities not reflected in the unit price but which would affect the rental bid of the hypothetical tenant.

Profits method

9.111   A profits method of valuation is appropriate, where the rental bid is based on the profit-earning capability of a *hypothetical tenant* in the actual property.

9.112   Use three years' accounts, valuing either as at the tone of the list, or date of proposal for public utilities, public houses or loss of trade since 1973. Adjust accounts to conform to statutory definitions and the hypothetical tenancy.

9.113   From gross receipts deduct working expenses (excluding rent, rates and repairs for gross value), from divisible balance deduct tenant's share. Remainder is rent and rates.

9.114   Include all plant and machinery as rateable.

Contractor's test

9.115   Interest on capital value or cost gives a guide to rental value, especially in cases of owner-occupation.

9.116   There are six stages:

(a)   Stage 1: cost of construction;
(b)   Stage 2: deductions to produce an effective capital value, or 'adjusted replacement cost';
(c)   Stage 3: add the cost of land (*rebus sic stantibus*);
(d)   Stage 4: apply appropriate rate of interest;
(e)   Stage 5: any further considerations, eg end allowances;
(f)   Stage 6: assess bargaining strengths of parties.

9.117 The contractor's test is not generally preferred to other methods of valuation.

Comparable assessments

9.118 Rating assessments of comparable hereditaments are used if better evidence is lacking, and to support other evidence. Over time, assessments in a list gain weight as evidence.

9.119 Assessments in the list are admissions of value by a valuation officer, but not an assessment under appeal.

9.120 The more unusual the hereditament, the further afield it is possible to go for evidence.

9.121 Refer to assessments anywhere for valuation practice and method. Always compare like with like.

Chapter 10

Valuation of selected property types

Synopsis

10.1 Having established whether a particular property is to be valued to gross value (7.8) or direct to net annual value (7.10), it is necessary to consider the methods of valuation which can be used.

10.2 In Chapter 9 the methods of valuation were outlined and an indication given of how rating principles adjust the normal application of those methods.

10.3 In *Garton* v *Hunter (VO)* (1968) it was established that the use of no one method is correct (unless the use of a statutory formula is required (9.8)), and that valuations by all methods of valuation are admissible in court proceedings (9.11–12).

10.4 In addition to the general principles of both rating and valuation which have been outlined in the three preceding chapters, the nature of the property type may affect the principles to be applied in a rating valuation.

10.5 This chapter indicates how the general principles of both rating and valuation are applied to specialist properties, and any unique features which such properties may possess will be considered in so far as they affect valuations for rating purposes.

The more usual properties (dwellings, shops, offices and industrial properties) are considered, together with certain other specialist properties, which illustrate how the methods of valuation are varied for the property type.

Dwellings

10.6 Dwellings are valued to *gross value* and, in the absence of adequate suitable *rental evidence*, valuations are based on *comparable rating assessments*.

10.7 With the government's proposals to phase out domestic rating over ten years from 1990, it is unlikely that dwellings will be the subject of a future revaluation. However, the problems encountered on a revaluation are explained, so that the basis established in the 1973 valuation list may be understood and used, for as long as it is relevant to the rating of dwellings.

10.8 With the growth of owner-occupation, the statutory control of the private rented sector and the judicial decision that statutorily controlled rents are not suitable as evidence for rating assessments (see 8.14), very few *suitable open-market rents exist*.

10.9 In 1976 the Layfield Report stated that the assessments of dwellings in the 1973 valuation list had been based on rents of less than two per cent of all dwellings, which highlights one of the major problems encountered in valuing dwellings on a revaluation.

10.10 This situation is aggravated by the fact that the term 'dwelling-house', which is used in the legislation, covers all types of residential accommodation, from mansions to caravans.

10.11 Within that range the courts have held, for example, that flats cannot be compared with houses (*Chritchlow* v *Almond (VO)* (1957)); bungalows with houses (*Dutton* v *Hall (VO)* (1966)); nor privately owned houses with council houses (*Garrod* v *Smith (VO)* (1965)); nor maisonettes with flats (*Berman* v *Playle (VO)* (1967)).

10.12 Because of the lack of rental evidence and the variety of dwelling types, the General Rate Act 1970 allowed as 'relevant and admissible' the following as evidence for the purposes of a revaluation:

(a) the rental evidence of dwellings of any description; and
(b) the relationship between those rents and the gross values of those dwellings in the previous valuation list;

provided that the dwellings are in the same, or a contiguous, valuation panel area.

10.13 As a result, for the purposes of creating the 1973 valuation list, evidence of rents passing on flats was 'relevant and admissible' in valuing a house in the same locality (generally, this meant the same county).

10.14 Similarly, the relationship between, for instance 1972 rents and 1963 gross values of, say, bungalows, can be used to value houses.

10.15 It is not, however, obligatory for the courts to adopt either rental evidence from other types of dwellings or the rent:gross value ratio. The General Rate Act 1970 only makes such evidence 'relevant and admissible', and allows valuation officers and the courts to use more reliable evidence, if it is available.

10.16 Once a valuation list has come into force and the tone of the list has been established, it is usual to base valuations of dwellings exclusively on rating assessments of *comparable dwellings* within the immediate locality.

10.17 In either case, it is usual to value dwellings as follows:

    (a) *basic gross value*, based on the *area* of the dwelling multiplied by a *unit price* per square metre: this is based on the value of that type of dwelling in that particular locality;

    (b) plus any *advantages* or additional facilities not reflected in the basic unit price;

    (c) less any *disadvantages* or disabilities normally expected in the basic unit price.

10.18 The area of the dwelling is normally measured to a *reduced covered area* (RCA). This is the gross external area of the property, including all walls and internal space. Flats, however, are measured to *effective floor area* (EFA), also known as 'carpet area'. This is the internal area of all habitable rooms (reception and bedrooms, usually including kitchen but excluding bathroom);

10.19 A *unit price* per square metre for each dwelling type will be established within each definable locality.

10.20 The unit price will depend on how the market evidence existing in any residential area reflects similarities or differences between dwellings of one type, say semi-detached houses, because of their age, construction or internal design, and because of their location, say close to or away from the main shopping centre.

10.21 It is, of course, essential to *compare like with like* and, despite the provisions of the General Rate Act 1970, rental evidence is preferred where available.

10.22 When comparison is impossible, for example where a modern house is built in an isolated location and no useful comparisons exist nearby, the courts may accept a 'spot' value.

Minor structural alterations

(*Local Government Act 1974, s 21*)

10.23 Because many people felt that when they improved their properties, they were penalised with increased rates, s 21(1) of the Local Government Act 1974 allowed some measure of relief when *minor structural alterations* are made to dwellings (see also 5.68–79).

10.24 Under the normal rules of rating, once structural alterations are carried out on a hereditament, the valuation officer, who has a duty to ensure that the valuation list is correct, should alter the list to take into account the structural alterations (assuming that they alter the rental value and, therefore, the rateable value and/or description of the hereditament). This is done by issuing a 'Proposal to alter the valuation list' as a result of which the appropriate entry in the list can be altered to take the structural alterations into account (see Chapters 7 and 12).

10.25 However, where only *minor structural alterations* (as defined in 10.26) are made to a dwellinghouse or *central heating* is installed in an occupied dwellinghouse, s 21(1) of the Local Government Act 1974 *prevents* anyone making a *proposal to increase the assessment* of that hereditament to take into account the structural alterations or central heating.

10.26 Under s 21(1)(*a*) of the Local Government Act 1974, in respect of a dwellinghouse or mixed hereditament (ie a hereditament comprising partly residential accommodation and partly any other use— see 5.96), 'no proposal may be made . . . for an increase in the gross value . . . by reason of the *making of structural alterations on or after 1 April 1974* . . . if the proposal would be for an *increase not exceeding . . .' £30*.

10.27 Minor structural alterations are thus defined by the Act (and the Rating of Minor Structural Alterations to Dwellings (Specified Amount) Order 1974) as including *alterations which do not increase the gross value of the hereditament by more than £30*. It is, therefore, a matter of valuation in any individual case as to what constitutes a minor structural alteration. It seems likely that a small kitchen extension or garage will be covered by this section.

10.28 Also, under s 21(1)(*b*) of the Local Government Act 1974, in respect of a dwellinghouse or mixed hereditament:

> no proposal may be made . . . for an increase in the gross value . . . by reason of the making of structural alterations on or after 1 April 1974 . . . if . . . the *alterations are necessary for the purpose*

of installing a system for providing heating in two or more rooms in the hereditament.

10.29 There is no value limit on the installation of central heating, so that any system installed after 1 April 1974 will not increase the gross value of the hereditament. However, additions to an existing heating system are not covered by this section and will therefore be taken into account in the gross value as normal (*Re Maudsley (VO) (1984)*).

10.30 Section 21 does not permit a valuer to ignore the effects of minor structural alterations or central heating but, after a normal valuation of the dwelling, s 21 prevents a proposal to increase the gross value by more than £30 or by any amount for central heating.

10.31 Thus, for example, if a garage were added to a dwellinghouse in 1980 and the increase in gross value were £20, no proposal may be made to increase the gross value because it would be for an amount not exceeding £30—precluded by s 21(1)(*a*) of the Local Government Act 1974. If, however, in 1984 a kitchen extension is added to the same dwellinghouse, which increases its gross value by £25, the overall increase in gross value which is not reflected in the valuation list will be £45 (£20 + £25), and a proposal *may* be made to increase an assessment by more than £30.

10.32 The reason statute prevents an increase in rate liability as a result of minor structural alterations of dwellinghouses is to encourage (or at least not discourage) home improvements which take the form of, for example, a kitchen or bathroom extension and the provision of central heating.

10.33 However, by limiting the relief to a procedural inability to increase the entry shown in the valuation list, and by not ignoring the increase in value altogether, the use of s 21(1) of the Local Government Act 1974 gave rise to *Dalby (VO)* v *Griffiths* (1976) and *Dalby (VO)* v *Lever* (1976) in which a reduction in gross value for a nuisance was claimed following the addition of central heating and an extension, covered by ss 21(1)(*a*) and (*b*) respectively.

10.34 In *Dalby (VO)* v *Griffiths* the court held that the provisions of s 21 did not affect the valuation of the hereditament, and that additions for central heating and structural alterations must be taken into account together with deductions for nuisance. Having arrived at a correct valuation, s 21 should be considered and the question asked: Will the proposal to give effect to the correct valuation increase the gross value by an amount exceeding £30? If the answer is no, the proposal is precluded by s 21 of the Local Government Act 1974, and the existing entry in the valuation list remains unaltered.

10.35 If the net result is a decrease in the existing gross value, a proposal may be made to give effect to that decrease, and s 21 has no effect in such case.

10.36 The valuation in *Dalby (VO)* v *Griffiths* was as follows (a gross value of £240 appeared in the valuation list prior to the appeal):

Basic gross value	£240
Plus: central heating (covered by s 21(1)(*b*) LGA 1974)	£20
Less: aircraft noise and local disturbance	£20
Gross value	£240

There was no alteration to existing gross value.

10.37 The valuation in *Dalby (VO)* v *Lever* was as follows (a gross value of £486 appeared in the valuation list prior to the appeal):

Basic gross value	£486
Plus: extension	30
Less: aircraft disturbance (5%)	24
Gross value	£492

There was no alteration to the existing gross value, since to do so would mean making a proposal for an increase of less than £30.

10.38 It is thus clear that s 21(1) does not affect the valuation, but merely what procedure can (or cannot) be followed once a correct value has been established.

Agricultural dwellinghouses

(GRA 1967, s 26(2), as amended by LGPLA 1980)

10.39 An agricultural dwellinghouse is *not* an 'agricultural building', and is not therefore exempted from rates (see also 5.63–7).

10.40 An *agricultural dwellinghouse* is *defined as* a house occupied in connection with agricultural land and used as the dwelling of a person who is primarily engaged in carrying on or directing agricultural or fish farming operations on that land or is employed in agricultural etc operations on that land in the service of the occupier of that land and is entitled to occupy the house only while so employed (s 26(2) as amended).

10.41 The usual method of valuation for a dwellinghouse is to assess a gross value (s 19(6)—see 7.11), ie:

the rent at which the hereditament might reasonably be expected to let from year to year if the tenant undertook to pay all usual tenants' rates and taxes and the landlord undertook to bear the cost of the repairs and insurance and the other expenses, if any, necessary to maintain the hereditament in a state to command that rent.

10.42 However, for as long as the house is occupied in connection with agricultural land and used as the dwelling of a person primarily engaged in or employed in agricultural operations on that land (see 10.40), it is classed as an agricultural dwellinghouse and its *gross value* is '*estimated by reference to the rent at which the house might reasonably be expected to let from year to year if it could not be occupied and used other than as aforesaid*' (s 26(2)).

10.43 The effect of this is to limit the rental bids which can be considered for the agricultural dwellinghouse to those payable by actual or potential occupiers engaged or employed in agricultural operations on agricultural land. This may depress the rent and thus the gross value, the rateable value (which is based on the gross value) and ultimately the rates paid.

10.44 The valuation proposed by the valuation officer in *Dunham* v *Bellamy (VO)* (1976) (in a case concerning state of disrepair) was as follows:

Basic gross value	
265m² at £1.40 per m²	£370
Plus: detached (5%)	18
	£388
Less: agricultural (s 26(2))(AG)(10%)	39
Gross value	£349
say	£350

Flats

10.45 Flats are just one type of dwelling and, as such, are valued to gross value on rental evidence where available, or on comparable assessments.

10.46 Flats may be purpose-built or converted within a building originally constructed for another purpose, eg a single dwellinghouse. Flats may be self-contained or non-self-contained.

10.47 With three exceptions, flats should be treated like other dwellings (see 10.6–44).

10.48 The first exception is that *more rental evidence* suitable for adjustment to gross value should be available for flats, because of the relative lack of statutory control on rents paid for flats.

10.49 Gross values for flats are, therefore, likely to be based on more reliable rental evidence than for other dwelling types.

10.50 The second exception is that flats are measured to *effective floor area*, EFA, also known as 'carpet area'. This is the internal area of all habitable rooms (reception and bedrooms, usually including kitchen but excluding bathroom).

10.51 The third exception is that s 23 will apply when flats are let at rents which include payments for *landlord's services* (see 9.39–41).

10.52 Thus, when adjusting the rent of flats on which to base a gross value, *no deduction should be made* for repair, replacement, maintenance and insurance of the common parts, landlord's profit in respect of such services, nor rent collection costs.

10.53 Deductions must, therefore, be limited to lighting, heating and cleaning of common parts, lifts, supervision, wages and insurance of staff involved in services.

Future valuation lists

10.54 Under the LGPLA 1980, for any future valuation list a *gross value* will be required only for a 'dwellinghouse', 'private garage' or 'private storage premises' (ie *domestic hereditaments*).

10.55 A 'dwellinghouse' is defined (s 115) as a hereditament which is used wholly for the purpose of a private dwelling or dwellings.

10.56 'Private garage' means a building having a floor space area not exceeding 25 square metres which is used wholly or mainly for the accommodation of a motor vehicle (1980 Act, s 29).

10.57 'Private storage premises' means a hereditament which is used wholly in connection with a dwellinghouse, and wholly or mainly for the storage of articles of domestic use (including bicycles and similar vehicles) belonging to the persons residing there. (1980 Act, s 29).

10.58 Also, under the 1980 Act provisions, the Secretary of State has the power to specify some hereditaments which are to be valued, while leaving the assessments of the *unspecified hereditaments* unaltered from those which appeared in the 1973 valuation list.

10.59 In addition, the Secretary of State may *adjust the rateable value* of either the specified or unspecified hereditaments in order to preserve the ratio which he estimates existed between the rateable values of specified and unspecified hereditaments prior to the coming into force of the new list.

10.60 In this way, it *might* be possible for the Secretary of State to ensure that no new revaluation of domestic hereditaments takes place. Instead, if domestic hereditaments are 'unspecified', the Secretary of State *could* 'adjust' the 1973 rateable values of all domestic hereditaments to preserve the ratio which exists between 'unspecified' and 'specified' hereditaments in the year prior to the introduction of the new list.

10.61 If this situation does arise, the rateable value of all domestic hereditaments in the new valuation lists will be based on their 1973 values, and all domestic hereditaments constructed during the life of any future list will be based on the 1973 tone of the list, as adjusted.

10.62 However, this likely use to which the provisions of the 1980 Act may be put is pure *speculation* at this stage, illustrating only one of several options available to the government when the decisions about the new lists are made.

Shops

10.63 Shops are valued to *gross value*, using *rental evidence*.

10.64 Shop rents may not be suitable evidence on which to base a gross value if the rent is paid under the Landlord and Tenant Act 1954 (as amended); where there is a user restriction which would not affect the hypothetical tenant; or where the rent was reduced to induce an anchor tenant to take space in a new development. (An anchor tenant is a department, variety, chain-store or supermarket whose presence encourages other potential tenants to rent units in the same development to take advantage of the customers the anchor tenant attracts).

10.65 An analysis should be made of the shopping centre in which the shop to be valued is situated, to identify patterns of value within the centre. Such patterns should be reflected in the rating assessments.

10.66 Having selected and adjusted rents to conform to gross value (see Chapter 9), the rents can be analysed to a unit of comparison.

10.67 Standard or normal shops (ie the typical shop type in the shopping centre) are analysed using the *zoning method*.

10.68 Large shops (such as supermarkets, superstores, departmental stores) may be more appropriately analysed to an *'overall' price per square metre*.

Zoning

10.69 Zoning is a method of analysis of ground floor sales area, which assumes that the front part of a shop in a busy high street is more valuable than the rear, due to its proximity to pavement traffic and the inducement it offers to window shoppers.

10.70 Having attracted potential customers into the shop, the front sales area is used to entice them deeper into the shop where purchases can be made.

10.71 The practical effect of this theory is that ground floor sales areas are divided into zones, with zone A (the most valuable zone) from the frontage back to a given depth; zone B, generally the same depth as zone A but only worth half as much; and zone C, which comprises the remainder of the ground floor sales area and is worth half as much as zone B. This relativity of values between the zones is called *halving back*. Ancillary accommodation is reflected as a fraction of zone A value.

10.72 The valuation officer uses an *arithmetic* or *arbitrary zoning method*, ie the depth of each zone (except the remainder) is known in advance, together with the relative values of any ancillary accommodation.

10.73 The depths of the zones and the relative values of any ancillary accommodation are based on local practice, although there are some locations where zoning is not used and a variant can be imposed (*British Home Stores Ltd* v *County Borough of Brighton and Burton (VO)* (1958)).

10.74 A typical variant is: zone A—6.1 metres; zone B—6.1 metres; zone C—remainder (also known as '20-foot zones'). The courts have also recognised: zone A—4.57 metres (15 feet); zone B—7.62 metres (25 feet); zone C—remainder; and zone A—18.29 metres (60 feet) with remainder.

10.75 As with any method of comparison, 'as you devalue, so you value', so that a comparison of 'like with like' is achieved.

10.76 A shop with a *return frontage* generally has a greater advantage over a similar shop without. In the absence of more direct evidence, a percentage addition (often ten per cent) is made to reflect the return frontage.

10.77 Where a shop has access on more than one frontage, it is accepted that zoning takes place from the most valuable frontage (*Watts (VO)* v *Royal Arsenal Co-operative Society Ltd* (1984)).

10.78 Where there is *ancillary accommodation* (eg stores, basement, first floor, offices etc), these are expressed as a fraction of the rental value of zone A, such fractions being either predetermined or based on rental evidence, but invariably worth less than any ground floor sales area.

10.79 A *quantity allowance* may be given if the assessment of a large shop is calculated using the rental evidence of small shops, because it is recognised that the two shop types are not truly comparable.

10.80 However, market evidence to support or reject a quantity allowance must be available, and the burden of proof rests on the appellant, whatever his point of view (*Trevail (VO)* v *C & A Modes Ltd* (1967)).

10.81 A quantity allowance is an allowance *for size* and should not be confused with an allowance *for shape*.

10.82 In *WH Smith & Son Ltd* v *Clee (VO)* (1977) the tribunal described an *allowance for size* as being an 'end allowance related to an overall size in all dimensions, to the extent (if any) that this factor may not already have been adequately allowed for in the values adopted for the various areas of floor space in the hereditament'.

10.83 This was contrasted with an *allowance for shape*, being 'an end allowance related to "size along the frontage" which . . . is incapable of reflection in the values adapted for the sales area . . .'

10.84 In recognising that it is normal to expect a frontage:depth ratio in the order of 1:2 or 1:3, the tribunal (in *WH Smith*) made an allowance for shape where the appeal hereditament had a ratio of 1:0.34.

10.85 As for a quantity allowance (or allowance for size), this should only be given if, and to the extent that, the market would not reflect the additional frontage and zone A space.

10.86 A *disability allowance* may be appropriate where shop properties suffer from such inconveniences as obsolete layout, obstructive pillars, inadequate or excessive height, lack of rear access, inadequate toilet facilities, absence of visibility from the main street, etc.

10.87 The principles of zoning do not apply to *large shops* because the frontage is of little or no importance as an inducement to attracting customers.

10.88 However, in the absence of the better rental evidence of truly comparable hereditaments, the zoning method of analysis allows assessments of large shops to be fixed using the rents of smaller shops. In *Trevail (VO)* v *C & A Modes Ltd* (1967) the court recognised an objective of zoning as being a means whereby the rating assessments of large shops could be reached by an examination of the rents of smaller shops.

10.89 It is, however, generally recognised that the zoning method of analysis is not satisfactory for large shops, and rental evidence of comparable large shops is preferred, even if this rental evidence appears as accepted rating assessments (*J Sainsbury* v *Wood (VO)* (1980)).

'Overall' method

10.90 Where rental evidence of large stores is available, it is expressed as a **price per square metre overall**, with ancillary accommodation being expressed as a fraction of that overall price and return frontages, disabilities etc being treated as for zoning (see 10.77–87).

10.91 In large shops, such as department stores, hypermarkets or supermarkets, it is generally recognised that one part of the ground floor sales area is worth no more than any other, and that a price per square metre overall can be justified.

10.92 However, the 'overall' method will be preferred to a zoning method only where reliable rental evidence exists to support both the method used and the price per square metre overall, and where the method of analysis has been tested in the market.

10.93 Comparable rating assessments have been treated as reliable rental evidence, correct at the time the valuation list came into force (*J Sainsbury* v *Wood (VO)* (1980)), but are more usually presented as evidence supporting a valuation based on actual rents.

10.94 Also valued in the same way as shops (ie zoned) are banks, restaurants, and shops used as offices (eg estate agent's or building society's premises).

10.95 The following is an example of shop **rental analysis** as produced in *Edma (Jewellers) Ltd* v *Moore (VO)* (1975). The valuation officer's analysis of rent was:

	£
Rent reserved (after initial 18 months at £4,500) for 5.5 years	5,250
Plus: annual equivalent of £18,000, ÷ YP 6% and 3% 21 years	1,714
	6,964
Plus: outgoings (5% external, 5% internal repairs)	696
	£7,660

Gross value   £7,500

10.96 In *FW Woolworth & Co Ltd* v *Moore (VO)* (1978) a Woolworth store was held on a full repairing and insuring lease at a 'shell' rent with 21-year reviews. The court established that the best starting point for valuation is the actual rent payable, with adjustments to reflect the fact that the rent fixed for 21 years is not the same as a rent 'from year to year'. The rent adjustment is shown in Table 10.96.

Table 10.96 Rent adjustment in Woolworth example

		£
Rent for 21 years		57,000
Less: difference between fixed rent for 21 years, and rent from year to year, say 15%		8,550
		48,450
Plus: estimated cost of finishings	315,000	
YP 6% and 3% 35 years	÷ 13	
Annual equivalent of capital expenditure		24,231
Net rental value		72,681
Plus: repairs, say 10%		7,268
Rent in terms of gross value		79,949

10.97 Table 10.97 gives an example of a valuation of shop with occupation disadvantages, using the zoning method of analysis (*Time Products Ltd (TAJ Weir & Sons Ltd) v Smith (VO)* (1983)).

Table 10.97 The zoning method with occupation disadvantages

	£
Ground floor:	
Zone A—43.9m² at £107.50 per m²	4,719
Zone B—25.0m² at £53.75 per m²	1,344
	6,063
Plus: return frontage (2.8%)	170
	6,233
Basement: storage (agreed)	779
	7,012
Disadvantages:	
Shape	
Ratio of frontage to depth	
Area of zone A to zone B	210
Not visible from the High Street (3%)	
Gross value	6,802
say	£6,800

10.98 Table 10.98 contains an example of the zoning method applied to a 'large' shop, as seen in *Watts (VO) v Royal Arsenal Co-operative Society Ltd* (1984), where zoning was adopted in preference to an 'overall' price per square metre for sales area, because all the main comparables were zoned, the zone A figure reflected the location factor more readily, and differences could be resolved 'fairly easily'. Zoning should be from the more valuable frontage.

Table 10.98   The zoning method applied to a large shop

			£	£
Ground floor				
Sales:				
Zone A—	297.5m² at 1	£36.0	10,710	
Zone B—	613.4m² at 1/2	£18.0	11,041	
Remainder	1,509.4m² at 1/4	£9.0	13,584	
	2,420.3m²			35,335
Ancillary:				
Cash office	29.5m² at 1/5	£7.2	212	
Butcher's shop/preparation	118.9m² at 1/6	£6.0	713	
Warehouse	616.2m² at 1/8	£4.5	2,772	
Fork-lift store	15.0m² at 1/10	£3.6	54	
Loading bay	375.0m² at 1/15	£2.4	900	
				4,651
First floor				
Ancillary:				
Offices	46.9m² at 1/5	£7.2	337	
Assistant manager	21.0m² at 1/6	£6.0	126	
Canteen/staff	148.5m² at 1/6	£6.0	891	
Stock	46.1m² at 1/8	£4.5	207	
Stock over boiler room	60.0m² at 1/10	£3.6	216	
				1,777
Total, say				41,760
Plus:				
Car park (3%)				1,253
Return frontage—19.5m at 1/2	£18.0			351
				43,365
Less:				
Size		12.5%		
Frontage/depth ratio		15%		11,925
				31,439
Less: excess height ('a little more than 1% of sales area')				439
Gross value				31,000

10.99   On future valuation lists, shop properties will be valued direct to net annual value.

Offices

10.100   Offices are valued to gross value, using rental evidence, reduced to a price per square metre of effective floor area.

10.101   Effective floor area may (or may not) include permanent partitions, but excludes staircases, lifts, landings etc.

Offices let as a single block

10.102   The hereditament comprises the whole block together with staircases, lifts, landings etc, and a gross value must be found for the whole.

10.103   If office premises are let to one tenant as a single block, it is likely that the terms of the lease will make the tenant responsible for all repairs, insurance and services, and any rent must be adjusted accordingly into terms of gross value.

Offices let in suites

10.104   The hereditaments will comprise each separately occupied suite of offices, with staircases, lifts, landings etc which are not in exclusive occupation not being part of any hereditament.

10.105   If an office block is let in suites to several tenants, it is likely that the terms of each lease will make the tenant responsible for internal repairs and decoration only, and any rent must be adjusted accordingly into terms of gross value.

10.106   The landlord may be liable for repairs to the structure, external decorations, insurance and services. When a rent paid under such terms is adjusted into terms of gross value, the effect of s 23 on landlord's services must be taken into account.

10.107   Under s 23, in deducting for *landlord's services*, no deduction should be made for repair, replacement, maintenance and insurance of common parts, landlord's profit in respect of such services, nor rent collection costs.

10.108   Deductions must, therefore, be limited to the costs of the lighting, heating and cleaning of common parts, lifts, supervision, wages and insurance of staff involved in services (see 9.39–41).

10.109   Offices are measured to *effective floor area*, which excludes staircases, lifts and landings. It may (or may not) also exclude permanent and demountable partitions, columns and stores, and it is therefore important to know the exact basis on which an office has been measured in order to 'compare like with like'.

Partitions

10.110   *Permanent partitions* are rateable as part of the physical structure of the building.

10.111 *Demountable* or *removable partitioning*, which is capable of being removed and relocated without any damage either to itself or to the main structure of the building, may or may not be rateable. Rateability will depend on the function such partitioning performs for the occupier.

10.112 Such partitioning may or may not be floor-to-ceiling height, require skilled fitters, be supplied by the tenant or in fact be frequently moved.

10.113 Demountable partitioning is either:

(a) part of the *setting* within which the business is carried out, in which case it forms part of the hereditament *and is rateable*; or

(b) *plant*, ie part of the businessman's apparatus for running his enterprise, *and not rateable*, because it is not listed (see 3.15–33); or

(c) *furniture*, being neither setting nor plant, *and not rateable*.

10.114 In order to determine whether or not demountable partitioning is rateable, consider the function it performs (*British Bakeries Ltd* v *Gudgion (VO) and Croydon LBC* (1969)).

10.115 If demountable partitions merely provide internal walls within which the business is carried on (a commercial convenience), they are setting and rateable as part of the hereditament. If they are necessary for the running of the business (a commercial necessity), they are plant and, not being listed in the relevant statutes, not rateable.

10.116 For a future valuation list, offices will be valued direct to net annual value.

Industrial property

10.117 Net annual value calculated direct is required for a hereditament which is used as a *factory*, *mill* or other premises of a similar character *used wholly or mainly for industrial purposes* (s 19).

10.118 All other hereditaments (except public utility undertakings' land, plant and machinery) are valued to gross value.

10.119 Thus, only premises which are actually *used* as a factory or mill can be valued *direct to net annual value*, and empty factories must be valued to gross value for as long as they remain empty (*Sheil (VO)* v *Borg-Warner Ltd* (1984)).

10.120 Similarly, any industrial hereditament the use of which fails to comply with the definition of 'factories, mills and other premises of a similar character used wholly or mainly for industrial purposes', such as *warehouses*, *workshops*, distribution depots etc must be valued to *gross value*.

10.121 Industrial property is valued using either the contractor's test or comparable rental evidence, depending on the nature of the property.

10.122 The *contractor's test* is used to value purpose-built industrial property which is put to a specialist use, since most are owner-occupied and rental evidence is either non-existent or of little help.

10.123 Examples of such properties are steelworks, cement works, oil refineries and chemical plants.

10.124 Much of the valuation of such hereditaments will involve *rateable plant and machinery* (see 3.15–33), with reliance being placed on the rental value of such items, assuming that they are provided by the landlord.

10.125 Special factors to be taken into account in the valuation of industrial properties are *economic obsolescence* caused by changes in the manufacturing process; a *limited capacity* in one part of the process which controls the output, despite surplus capacity elsewhere; and *trading conditions* which affect the particular industry and which may affect the capacity at which it is reasonable to operate the unit (*Sheerness Steel Co plc* v *Maudling (VO)* (1986)).

10.126 The majority of industrial properties can normally be valued using *rental evidence*, because there is usually a sufficient supply of suitable, reliable rents available.

10.127 Such properties are usually measured to *effective floor area* (net internal area) and a price per square metre (adjusted to either gross or net annual value, as appropriate) applied.

10.128 Items of rateable *plant and machinery* must also be valued as part of the hereditament, care being taken to ensure that if the price per square metre assumes certain rateable plant (for example central heating), there is not another addition made for that plant in the valuation (see 3.15–33).

10.129 Factors to be taken into account include the *height* of the unit; *floor loading capacity* in relation to the intended use; ease of manoeuvrability for *fork-lift trucks* and other moving machinery; loading/unloading facilities; *accessibility* to vehicular and/or rail transport facilities, unrestricted by vehicular weight limitations or low bridges; availability of a suitable *labour force*; and *public services* etc.

10.130 Because rental evidence may indicate that there is little or no demand for factory units above a certain size, a *quantity allowance* may be made to allow for the space which is in excess of the needs of the hypothetical tenant (see 10.79–80).

10.131 *Key Terrain Ltd* v *Gerdes (VO)* (1986) involved the valuation of an ultra-modern, high-specification building of good quality, where the valuation shown in Table 10.131 was confirmed.

Table 10.131 Valuation of Key Terrain's industrial building

		£
Main factory	3,675.9m² at £5.25 per m²	19,298
Loading bays (2)	91.2m² at £5.50 per m²	502
Offices	148.1m² at £5.75 per m²	852
Locker room and ancillaries	109.8m² at £2.75 per m²	302*
2 Compressors—£2,000 at 5% (to NAV)		100*
		21,054
Less: end allowance (ramped access) (4.5%)		967
		20,087
Existing assessment (figure in valuation list as at date of VO's proposal)		96,250
Rateable value		116,337
	say	£116,320

* Agreed values

Plant and machinery

(See also 3.15–33.)

10.132 Some items of rateable plant and machinery are valued as part of the building in which they exist, eg items concerned with heating, lighting, ventilating, drainage, supplying with water etc.

10.133 However, when an item of rateable plant and machinery which is listed under *Class 1B* is used in the *manufacturing process*, *operations* or *trade*, it ceases to be rateable.

10.134 Class 1B lists as exempt in this way any item specified in Table 1B which is used or intended to be used mainly or exclusively in connection with the heating, cooling, ventilating, draining or supplying of water to the land or building . . . or protecting the hereditament from fire.

10.135 Where rateable plant and machinery is a separate hereditament, it is valued to *net annual value direct*, by ascertaining an *effective*

capital value for the item and applying an appropriate *percentage* (generally between five and six per cent) to reduce it to annual terms.

10.136 Particularly with items of plant and machinery, economic obsolescence must be considered as well as the relationship between *in situ* value and replacement costs.

10.137 The valuation officer may be asked to supply a list of all items of rateable plant and machinery which have been included in an assessment (s 21(2)), but he is not obliged to give details of how he has valued those items.

10.138 For a future valuation list all industrial properties, including warehouses and unused industrial premises, will be valued direct to net annual value.

Petrol filling stations

10.139 Depending on the nature of the hereditament, a petrol filling station is valued *either to gross or net annual value*. The more offices, workshops, showrooms etc on the hereditament, the more likely it is that the hereditament will require a gross value.

10.140 Petrol filling stations are valued on the *throughput*, ie the volume of petrol sold, together with *rental evidence* for all ancillary accommodation.

10.141 The hypothetical tenant for a petrol filling station is either an individual prepared to run the station as a going concern, or a petrol company which wants to secure the station as a retail outlet for its products and install its own tenant.

10.142 The rental bids of both such hypothetical tenants must be considered for the hereditament.

10.143 The actual rent which is paid for a petrol filling station is unlikely to be of much use in fixing a gross or net annual value if it is a 'tied' rent.

10.144 Petrol filling stations are often owned by petrol companies who let the stations at a rent which ties the tenant to a particular brand of product.

10.145 This rent cannot be used to fix a gross or net annual value, since the hypothetical tenant pays a rent which is not tied in any way.

10.146 Petrol companies are likely to be more interested in renting stations with a high 'throughput' and little ancillary accommodation than one with a low 'throughput' and a lot of ancillary accommodation.

10.147 Where appropriate, the 'overbid' of a petrol company should be recognised in the rental value.

10.148 It is, therefore, the factors which affect the gross profit to be made from the sale of a litre of petrol which will affect the rental value, together with the additional manufacturer's profit if there is to be a petrol company's 'overbid'.

10.149 Such factors include the use of inducements, eg glasses, coupons and trading stamps, the hours worked by the tenant, and the variety and quality of petrol sold.

10.150 The size of the petrol tanks is also relevant. If they are relatively large, the hypothetical tenant may benefit from a reduction in the unit cost by purchasing his petrol in bulk. If the tanks are relatively small, more frequent deliveries are necessary and the hypothetical tenant will incur extra delivery charges.

10.151 However, only if the petrol tanks are encased in solid concrete will they be rateable as listed plant. Other items which are likely to be exempt as items of plant and machinery which are not listed are the petrol pumps and recording consoles.

10.152 In any case, the pits into which the tanks are sunk are rateable as part of the setting.

10.153 Valuing the hereditament *rebus sic stantibus* means observing the actual hours of opening, and not assuming a greater throughput on the basis of potentially longer opening hours.

10.154 To the adjusted throughput, a figure per 1,000 litres is applied to obtain a rent for the 'forecourt element'. The rent for any buildings, such as showrooms, lubricating bays etc, is added to the rent for the 'forecourt element' to produce a gross or a net annual value.

10.155 For a fuller discussion, reference should be made to *The Valuation and Development of Petrol Filling Stations* by Sedgwick and Westbrook—see Bibliography.

10.156 For a future valuation list, petrol filling stations will be valued direct to net annual value.

Cinemas and theatres

10.157 Cinemas and theatres are valued to **gross value** using the **profits method** of valuation.

10.158 The profits method is used because of the lack of rental evidence for such properties and the element of monopoly which their licence gives them.

10.159 Annual admission receipts are calculated by estimating the average number of full houses a cinema achieves.

10.160 Together with admission charges, gross income includes receipts from the sale of refreshments, screen advertising and car parking charges (if any).

10.161 Factors which affect actual income include the circumstances of the actual occupier. This may be a company forming part of a large group which is able to reduce costs by economies of scale. Group management may distort the accounts and, therefore, the profitability of any one cinema. This should be ignored for rating purposes, when it must be assumed that the hypothetical tenant is renting only one hereditament.

10.162 In *Thorn EMI Cinemas Ltd* v *Harrison (VO)* (1986) the parties took the gross receipts achieved in 1982. These were adjusted to values as at 1 April 1973 by a factor derived from comparison between 1973 and 1982 seat prices (which was broadly comparable with the movement of the Retail Prices Index).

10.163 To the adjusted gross receipts, an appropriate rate per cent was applied to produce a gross value.

10.164 In this case, the tribunal stated that the volume of trade as at the date of the proposal was not to be disregarded in a s 20 (tone of the list) valuation:

> The value of most if not all premises which are used for commercial purposes . . . must depend in a broad sense upon the volume of trade or business carried on, and in arriving at the notional value of such premises on the artificial assumptions to be found in s 20 it is quite impossible to exclude the element of value attributable to the volume of trade or business.

10.165 In *Thorn EMI Cinemas Ltd* v *Harrison (VO)* (1986) an ABC cinema purpose-built in the 1930s had been converted in the early 1970s to twin cinemas with seating capacities of 600 and 373. Occupancy in 1973 had been 30 per cent but was down to 12 per cent in 1982.

> Actual gross receipts (1982)   £260,655
> Adjusted to 1 April 1973*   £90,000
> Rate per cent applied   8.5%
> Gross value   £7,650 (ie £7.86 per seat)

* Adjustment to 1 April 1973 is achieved by applying to the actual 1982 gross receipts a factor derived from a comparison between 1973 and 1982 seat prices (broadly comparable with the movement of the Retail Prices Index).

10.166 This valuation used last accounts available prior to the date of the proposal (1982) because s 20 (tone of the list) valuations were lower than s 19 (gross value as at the date of the proposal) valuations.

10.167 According to the court, volume of trade is *not* to be disregarded by s 20 (tone of the list) (see 10.164).

10.168 For a future valuation list, cinemas and theatres will be valued direct to net annual value.

Licensed property

10.169 Licensed property is valued to *gross value* using the *direct approach method*, a variation of the profits method.

10.170 When licensed property is valued during the life of a valuation list s 20 (tone of the list) does not apply, and the appropriate accounts to be used are the latest accounts available at the date of the proposal.

10.171 The hypothetical tenant of licensed property is renting not only the property with its profit-making capabilities, but also the monopoly which the on-licence gives it.

10.172 For this reason, a hypothetical tenant may be an individual or a brewery. In fact, many licensed properties are owned by breweries who 'tie' their public houses to purchase all drinks from their own breweries.

10.173 Rent paid for such 'tied' public houses is, therefore, of little use in fixing a gross value, since the hypothetical tenant does not occupy under 'tied' conditions.

10.174 In recognition of the brewery's interest in renting public houses, any potential *overbid* should be established and quantified by market evidence (*Robinson Bros (Brewers) Ltd* v *Durham County Assessment Committee* (1938)).

10.175 When valuing licensed property as the result of a proposal to alter the valuation list (ie not on a revaluation), tone of the list (s 20) does not apply to the 'wet' trade. The volume of trade or business carried on at a public house is specified as a 'relevant factor' to be taken into account as at the date of the proposal (s 20).

10.176 Where accounts are used, therefore, they should be the latest accounts available to the hypothetical tenant at the date of the proposal.

10.177 The *direct approach* method assumes that the brewer is the hypothetical tenant who will sublet to a 'tied' tenant.

10.178 It is first necessary to estimate the *future maintainable trade* in drinks, ie the 'wet' trade. This is the level of trade maintainable by a typical hypothetical tenant, not the actual tenant, although the actual level of trade may be used as a guide.

10.179 From the volume of the 'wet' trade the profit made can be estimated.

10.180 To this profit is added the *tied rent* which a brewery would receive. The tied rent reflects the running costs, living accommodation and any other facilities or capabilities, except 'amusement with prizes machines'.

10.181 In addition, part of the profits from the *amusement with prizes machines* (gaming machines) also increases the rent paid to the hypothetical landlord.

10.182 Since many licensed properties also provide food ('dry' trade), a percentage of the profits achieved by the *'dry' trade* is also included in the rent to be paid, ie the gross value.

10.183 The percentage applied to the 'wet' trade is not necessarily the same as the percentage applied to the 'dry' trade.

10.184 In *Couper (VO)* v *Aylesbury Brewery Co Ltd* (1985) a public house and wine bar was situated on a corner site in a shopping centre. The direct method was used for both the public house (where the bulk of the trade was 'wet') and the wine bar (where the bulk of the trade was 'dry', ie catering). The calculations are shown in Table 10.184.

Table 10.184 The direct method applied to a public house and wine bar

		£
Brewer's profit:		
Draught beer—550 barrels at £5.00		2,750
Bottled beer—50 barrels at £6.50		325
Wines and spirits—2,000 gallons at £0.90		1,800
Total brewer's profit		4,875
Plus: estimated tied rent based on the 'wet' trade		3,487
		8,362
Brewer's bid (50% of £8,362)	£4,181	
2 gaming machines	225	
Rent for 'wet' trade and 'amusement with prizes machines'		4,406
Plus: catering turnover (net of VAT)		
1980/81	£142,500	
Adjusted to 1973 RPI factor (0.33)	47,025	
Appropriate rate per cent (10%)		4,702
Gross value		9,108
	say	£9,000

10.185 Where a licensed property is not owned by (and, therefore, 'tied' to) a brewery, the direct approach method is adapted so that there is no brewer's overbid and the hypothetical tenant is the licensee.

10.186 For a future valuation list, all licensed property will be valued direct to net annual value.

10.187 For a fuller discussion, reference should be made to *The Valuation of Licensed Premises* by Westbrook—see Bibliography.

Schools

10.188 Because of the difference in funding, schools are treated differently, depending on whether they are:

(a) county and voluntary schools (funded by local authorities);
(b) private schools (funded from other sources).

County and voluntary schools

10.189 Despite the statutory power (s 30) given to the Secretaries of State for Environment and Education to make regulations to assess schools on a formula basis, no regulations exist to date; such schools are valued to **gross value** on a recognised **non-statutory formula** derived from the contractor's test.

10.190 Because it is **non-statutory**, it is not possible to rely on the formula alone at court proceedings. There must be other evidence, such as a valuation on the contractor's basis or comparable rating assessments, on which the court can judge the results of the formula.

10.191 In *Dawkins (VO) v Royal Leamington Spa Corporation and Warwickshire County Council* (1961) the court said that the use of a non-statutory formula 'was a convenient short-cut, the use of which a valuation officer could indicate by proving the correctness of a particular assessment by a valuation on the contractor's basis . . . the only valid test'.

10.192 It is, therefore, not enough to follow the non-statutory formula and expect the courts to accept the valuation. The gross value contended for must be proved with evidence just like any other valuation.

10.193 In *Shrewsbury School (Governors) v Hudd* (1966) the tribunal preferred the contractor's test to a valuation based on a value per pupil place, although such a figure could be useful as a check, or for comparison between schools.

10.194 In recognition of the fact that local authorities are hypothetical tenants for such premises, the courts have adopted five per cent as a suitable rate to apply to the effective capital value of the land and buildings.

The non-statutory formula for county and voluntary schools assumes a basic price per scholar place according to the type of school and basic facilities. Thus, for a middle school, the basic price per scholar place is £21.50 assuming a 'normal' site value and certain basic facilities, eg hall. Thus, the method of calculating the gross value would be as shown in Table 10.194.

Table 10.194   The non-statutory formula for county and voluntary schools

Basic price per scholar place	£21.50
('Normal' site value and assuming certain basic facilities, eg hall.)	
Number of scholar places:	
Net internal class space (assuming a standard area per scholar of 2.7m²)	
Basic GV per scholar place	
	£
Less: disabilities including:	
Age and obsolescence (within a range from pre-1875, 80%, to 1945–1959, 10%)	
Absence of services	
Plus: ancillary accommodation including kitchens etc	
Total	
Superfluity allowance	
$\dfrac{\text{Registered number}}{\text{Standard capacity}} \times \text{Total} =$	
Plus: caretaker's house, community centre etc	
Gross value	

Privately funded schools

10.195   These are generally valued in the same way as county or voluntary schools, ie using the contractor's test, although the non-statutory formula is inappropriate and there may be rental evidence available.

10.196   In recognition of the likely hypothetical tenants of such premises, the courts have adopted a rate of 3.5 per cent to be applied to the effective capital value of land and buildings (*Eton College* v *Lane (VO) and Eton UDC* (1971)).

Caretaker's house

10.197   Provided that the caretaker's house is within or contiguous to the curtilage of the school, the house will be assessed as part of the school and its gross value (calculated normally) included in the gross value of the school assessment.

10.198   The description of the hereditament should indicate that this is the case.

10.199   In fact, it is the occupier of the school itself (either the local education authority or the school board of governors) who is the rateable occupier of such premises if the caretaker's house is occupied under a service tenancy.

10.200   In *Eton College* v *Lane (VO) and Eton RDC* (1971) the college comprised buildings that were old and were less than ideal for use as a large boarding house.

10.201   The building to be replaced was not a 'simple substitute' but a new building of the same size, shape, height and visual appearance, but without any architectural embellishments and extravagances, and having the same internal design. The calculation is shown in Table 10.201.

10.202   For a future valuation list, all schools will be valued direct to net annual value.

Colleges and universities

10.203   Colleges and universities are valued to **gross value** using the normal **contractor's test**.

10.204   In *Imperial College of Science and Technilogy* v *Ebdon (VO) and Westminster City Council* (1984) both parties presented valuations based on the five stages recognised in *Gilmore (VO)* v *Baker-Carr* (1963), but the Lands Tribunal amended this and added a sixth stage, shown in Table 10.205.

10.205   Thus, valuations for colleges and universities follow the normal contractor's test, as illustrated in 9.82–96.

10.206   For a future valuation list, colleges and universities will be valued direct to net annual value.

Table 10.201   The Eton College calculation

		£
Buildings:		
Estimated replacement cost (modern materials) of original buildings		4,600,000
Less: allowance for age and obsolescence, say 63%*		2,898,000
Effective capital value		1,702,000
Site:		
22.67 ha at £17,910 per ha	£406,000	
Less: 63%*	£256,000	
		150,000
Effective capital value land and buildings		1,852,000
Playing fields:		
80 ha at £1,063/ha		85,000
Total effective capital value		1,937,000
Appropriate rate per cent 3.5%		
3.5% of £1,937 000 is	£67,793	
Less: end allowance (10%)	£6,780	
Gross value		61,013
	say	£61,000

* In the *Imperial College* case (1985) the tribunal said that the amount of the deduction to be made from the buildings was *not necessarily* the same as that which should be made from the land.

Caravans

(See also 3.9.)

10.207   Caravans are chattels and, as such, are not rateable.

10.208   However, if a caravan is located on land for more than twelve months and its use enhances the enjoyment of that land, it will be rateable together with that land (*Field Place Caravan Park Ltd* v *Harding (VO)* (1966)).

10.209   Various situations can arise with caravans which require different considerations.

Table 10.205   The six stages of the contractor's test

	£
Stage I: Estimated replacement cost of buildings Estimated replacement cost of modern substitute buildings (12 units)	20,340,438
Stage II: Adjusted replacement cost Not effective capital value! Cost adjusted by 11% (approx) to allow for the actual state of the existing buildings; it was not a conversion into value. Factors considered were design, height, noise, heating	18,099,355
Stage III: Effective capital value of land Deductions from 'cost' of buildings may not be appropriate for 'value' of land—consider facts of each case	5,598,100
Total for land and buildings	23,697,455
Stage IV: Decapitalisation rate Real rate of interest plus borrower's premium plus depreciation and repair: 3.5% of £23,697,455	829,411
Stage V: Overall considerations Matters not already accounted for, eg difficulties of goods access to site, effects and inflexibility of district heating scheme: 7.5%	62,206
	767,205
Stage VI: The negotiations Is this figure likely to be pushed up or down in the negotiations between hypothetical landlord and hypothetical tenant, having regard to the relative bargaining strength of the parties? Not in this case.	
Gross value, say	767,000

Caravans used as dwellings

10.210   Where a caravan is used as a dwelling, it is valued to **gross value** using **rental evidence**.

10.211   *Comparable assessments* of other caravans and prefabricated bungalows may be useful (*Leighton* v *Thomas (VO)* (1977)).

10.212   It may, however, be necessary to value the land using rental evidence and the caravan using the contractor's test (*Stout* v *Capstick (VO)* (1978)).

10.213   Where such hereditaments are located on a commercially organised site, and where other property, such as shops, site offices, washing blocks etc are situated within the site, these site facilities will form a separate *(residual) hereditament* valued direct to *net annual value*, using rental evidence and/or comparable assessments (*Rye Bay Caravan Park Ltd* v *Morgan (VO)* (1979)).

10.214 The site operator will be the rateable occupier of the remainder of the site and its facilities.

'Leisure' caravans (See also 4.44–50.)

10.215 Because of the rate collection problems associated with caravans left permanently on a site but occupied only for part of the year, the Rating (Caravan Sites) Act 1976 gives the valuation officer discretion either to assess each pitch and caravan and the site facilities as *separate hereditaments* (as above), or to assess the whole site with all the caravans as a *single hereditament* in the rateable occupation of the site operator.

10.216 For the Rating (Caravan Sites) Act 1976 to apply, leisure caravans must be located on a site of not less than 400 square yards (334 square metres), covered by a planning restriction which prevents the occupation of the caravans during the whole year, and in which, but for the 1976 Act, each van and pitch would comprise a separate hereditament.

10.217 If the whole site is assessed as one hereditament, the site operator (the rateable occupier) must comply with the provisions in the Act relating to the display etc of details of the assessment.

10.218 Such a hereditament is valued direct to *net annual value* (Rating (Caravan Sites) Act 1976, s 1(4)).

Site for touring caravans

10.219 Where land is used for the parking of touring caravans, the site operator is likely to be rateable for the land and any site facilities.

10.220 Such a site is likely to be valued direct to *net annual value* and, following the decision in *Garton* v *Hunter (VO)* (1968) which concerned the assessment of a caravan site, *any method of valuation* is admissible as evidence to the courts.

Caravan within the curtilage of a dwelling

10.221 If a caravan, kept within the curtilage of a dwelling, is used in conjunction with that dwelling as living space, the assessment of the hereditament will include the advantages offered by the caravan.

10.222   If, however, the caravan is kept within the curtilage but used only elsewhere, eg as a touring caravan, the caravan itself will not increase the rental value of the dwelling.

10.223   However, the ability to keep a caravan within the curtilage of the dwelling may be something which should be reflected in the assessment of that dwelling.

10.224   For a future valuation list, all commercial properties will be valued direct to net annual value with only 'domestic hereditaments' (including dwellings) valued to gross value.

Hotels

10.225   Hotels are valued to *gross value* using either *rental evidence* (where available), a *profits method* of valuation, or (where appropriate) comparable assessments.

10.226   In estimating the gross income, it may be convenient to analyse the relative values attached to the bedrooms to produce a 'reduced bedroom' capacity.

10.227   Thus, if a hotel has ten bedrooms, six worth twice as much as the other four, the hotel has eight 'reduced bedrooms' to which a unit value can be applied.

10.228   It is necessary to allow a sinking fund to replace the tenant's furniture and equipment in addition to the tenant's share.

10.229   The valuations submitted to the Tribunal in *Strand Hotels Ltd v Hampsher (VO)* (1977) are shown in Tables 10.229 and 10.230.

10.230   The valuation submitted by the valuation officer appears in Table 10.230.

10.231   However, in *Central Hotels (Cranston) Ltd v Ridgeon (VO)* (1977) the gross value of a hotel was decided solely on the evidence of a comparison with the assessments of nine other hotels in the immediate locality.

10.232   For a future valuation list, commercial properties will be valued direct to net annual value.

Table 10.229 Valuation submitted by ratepayers—Strand Hotels

		Room rate £	Daily rate £
Estimated gross income:			
Rooms:			
Singles	104	10.50	1,092
Twin/double	712	14.50	10,324
Suites:			
2 rooms	6	27.00	162
3 rooms	2	45.00 (Av)	90
Total	824		11,668
For annual rate			× 365
			4,258,820
Estimated occupancy: 50%			2,129,400
Catering, banqueting and bars:			
Take 2/3 of room income			1,419,600
Total estimated gross income from year to year			3,549,000
			£
Less: estimated expenditure			
(a) For cost of sales and working expenses, allow 80% of gross income			2,839,200
(b) For renewal fund for tenant's long-life capital			112,500
			2,951,700
Divisible balance			597,300
Less: tenant's share:			
(a) Interest on tenant's capital: 1,572,700 at 12%			188,700
(b) Remuneration or share of profit at 60% of difference for substantial risk involved			245,200
			433,900
Gross value plus rates			163,400
Less: Rates payable £96,055 at 50p			48,000
Gross value of completed hereditament			115,400
Gross value, say			£115,000

Table 10.230   Valuation submitted by valuation officer—Strand Hotels

Description	No. of units/ area		Pricing		£
Main bedroom accommodation:					
Single bedrooms	104	at	£375 ea		39,000
Double bedrooms	688	at	£600 ea		412,800
Double bedrooms (large)	24	at	£675 ea		16,200
Penthouse suites:					
Two-roomed suites	6	at	£1,350 ea		8,100
Three-roomed suites	2	at	£1,950 ea		3,900
Total	824				480,000
Ancillary parts:					
Restaurants, bar, conference rooms, sales counters, kitchen stores etc	3963.7m²	at	£50 per m²		198,185
					678,185
Car Park					
90 Spaces at £50 per car					4,500
					682,685
Staff hostel:					
Staff bedrooms	95	at	£175	16,250	
Flat				say £250	
Recreation rooms	52.15m²	at	£20 per m²	17,957	
				say	700,600
Less: parts incapable of occupation:					
Single bedrooms	26	at	£375 ea	9,750	
Double bedrooms	228	at	£600 ea	136,800	
Double bedrooms (large)	8	at	£675 ea	5,400	
Penthouse suites:					
Two-roomed suites	5	at	£1,350 ea	6,750	
Three-roomed suites	2	at	£1,950 ea	3,900	
Total	269				162,600
					538,000

Less: excess of staffing requirements to unfinished hotel during contract period, continuing development of locality and general environmental disabilities, say 20%

	107,600
	£430,400
Gross value, say	£430,000

Chapter 11

The valuation list

Synopsis

11.1 All hereditaments which are valued are entered into the valuation list, and it is the rateable values contained in the valuation list on which the rating authority levies rates.

11.2 The duty to maintain a correct list belongs to the valuation officer, who will revalue all specified hereditaments when an order for a revaluation is made by the Secretary of State for the Environment. (The requirement for quinquennial revaluations has been abolished.)

11.3 The list is kept by the rating authority, which alters it on direction from the valuation officer. There is a separate list for each rating area.

11.4 The valuation list is altered by way of a proposal to alter the valuation list.

The statutory requirement

11.5 Section 67(1) of the General Rate Act 1967 provides that for the purpose of rates there shall be maintained for each rating area a valuation list, prepared, and from time to time altered (in accordance with Part V of the 1967 Act), by the valuation officer.

11.6 The *valuation officer* is an officer charged with the statutory duty of bringing a valuation list into existence and maintaining it in correct and legal form. He is appointed by the Commissioners of Inland Revenue, and is more fully defined in s 115(1) as:

>   . . . in relation to a valuation list, a rating area of any premises . . . any officer of the Commissioners who is for the time being appointed by the Commissioner to be the valuation officer or one of the valuation officers, or to be the deputy valuation officer or

one of the deputy valuation officers, in relation to that list . . . in which those premises are situated, as the case may be.

11.7 Section 68(1) of the GRA 1967 prescribed that new valuation lists should be made for all rating areas every five years. (The list currently in force took effect on 1 April 1973.) Section 1 of the General Rate Act 1975 postponed the first quinquennial revaluation and provided for the Secretary of State to make, by order, further postponements of one year.

11.8 Section 68(1) has been amended by s 28 of the LGPLA 1980, which abolishes the requirement for quinquennial revaluations and substitutes a requirement that *new valuation lists* for every rating area shall be prepared and made by valuation officers so as to come into force on 1 April in such year as the Secretary of State for the Environment may specify by order. Such an order must be approved by Parliament. (New valuation lists are due to take effect on 1 April 1990.)

11.9 Under ss 67(2) and 113(1)(*a*), the valuation list must be in the form prescribed by the Valuation Lists Rules 1972 (or in a form substantially to the like effect). It must contain particulars (subject to certain exceptions) of every hereditament in the rating area and its value, and totals of values in respect of the whole rating area and any rating district (ie an area within a rating area subject to differential rating).

11.10 Except for agricultural hereditaments and the railway, canal, sewer and land drainage hereditaments, all exempt hereditaments are to be entered in the list, but while the occupier is wholly exempt from payment no values may be entered against them.

11.11 However, where the exemption relates to Crown occupation, the value on which the amount of the Crown contribution in lieu of rates is computed is entered as representing the rateable value.

11.12 All these may be entered as a separate group in the valuation list under the heading 'Exemptions (contribution cases)'.

11.13 The main part of the valuation list (Section I) is split into columns requiring the following information: an assessment number, an analysis code, description, address, gross value, rateable value and a reference column for amendments (see Appendix 4, item 7).

11.14 The *assessment number* is a unique thirteen-digit figure which identifies the hereditament. The *analysis code* is a four-digit figure which will identify the type of hereditament, eg dwellinghouse, shop, hospital, racecourse etc, and is required for statistical analysis.

11.15 The *description* must accurately reflect the hereditament (any error in the entry is a ground for altering the list). The *address* must be accurate to the extent that there is no doubt as to the hereditament involved.

11.16 The *gross value* (if one is required) must be entered, and the *rateable value* is the figure on which rates are paid.

11.17 The final column, for amendments, will refer to the location in the list of any *direction* made to alter a particular entry. Prefaced by the letter 'D', the reference number will give the page and line of any altered entry relating to that particular hereditament which is contained in Section II of the list (see 12.78 and Appendix 4, item 8).

11.18 In addition, there are pages (Section III) giving totals of all rateable values for each rating district and area, including separate totals for gas and electricity hereditaments, so that at any given time a rating authority knows the total rateable values in its area on which rates are to be levied (see Appendix 4, item 9).

Local Government Planning and Land Act 1980

11.19 The LGPLA 1980 inserts two new sections (ss 19A and 19B) into the 1967 Act, which give the Secretary of State power to specify classes of hereditaments which are to be the subject of revaluation, and to specify a **valuation date** for those valuations. He also has the power to adjust the rateable values of those unspecified classes of hereditaments which are not subject to a revaluation, but which are included in a new valuation list.

11.20 Section 19A provides for an *antecedent valuation date*. When a new valuation list comes into force on 1 April in any year, the Secretary of State may specify an earlier time by reference to which valuations for net annual value are to be made for certain specified hereditaments. This will obviate the problem of predicting values which should exist on the date when the list comes into force. (Note that this section will only take effect when a new list comes into force and only if the Secretary of State makes an order to this effect.)

11.21 Where such an order is made and the valuation is carried out as at an earlier specified date, it must be based on the assumptions laid down in s 19A(2), ie:

  (a) that the hereditament is in the same state as at the time the list comes into force;
  (b) that the 'relevant factors' (see GRA 1967, s 20) are those subsisting at the time the list comes into force;

(c) that the state of the locality, transport and other facilities, and other matters affecting amenity are all as at the time the list comes into force.

11.22 Any order made under s 19A will affect only 'a specified hereditament', ie a hereditament of a class specified in the order. For any *hereditament which is not specified*, the net annual value in the new list will be the same as that in the valuation list in force immediately preceding the new list.

11.23 Section 19B empowers the Secretary of State to issue an order to prescribe a method of *adjusting the rateable values* so that the ratio which existed in the previous valuation list between the rateable values of specified and unspecified hereditaments is preserved.

11.24 It is therefore *possible* for the Secretary of State to specify that a new valuation list will come into force on 1 April 1990, and that all hereditaments except domestic hereditaments shall be specified. This will mean that, with the exception of domestic hereditaments, all other hereditaments are specified and must therefore be valued normally.

11.25 It will then be *possible* for the Secretary of State to allow that the 1973 rateable values of all domestic hereditaments (the only ones to be valued to gross value at this time) be adjusted, perhaps by a multiplier, and inserted in the 1990 list at the resultant figures.

11.26 This should give the Secretary of State total control over the spread of the rate burden between domestic and commercial ratepayers.

Rent returns

(*Section 82 of the GRA 1967*—see 12.81 and Appendix 4, item 10.)

11.27 For the purposes of a revaluation the valuation officer may serve a notice on the occupier, owner or lessee of any hereditament or premises in the area, requiring him to make a return containing '*such particulars as may be reasonably required for the purpose of enabling him accurately to compile the list*' (s 82(1)). It is at the discretion of the valuation officer whether he will call for the return from the occupier, the owner or the lessee, or from one or more of them.

11.28 A valuation officer may also call for a s 82 rent return in order to decide whether to make a proposal or to object to a proposal (see Chapter 12).

11.29 Such particulars include:

(a) name of occupier and date from which occupation first began;

(b) a description of the premises: shop, shop with living accommodation, office, factory etc;

(c) nature of the trade, business, or profession carried on;

(d) amount of rent now payable;

(e) does rent include: rates, external repairs, internal repairs,
insurance, heating, lighting, other services provided by the
landlord, the use of trade fixtures, fittings, plant and
machinery?

(f) does the rent relate to the whole property?

(g) when did the rent first become payable?

(h) is the rent subject to variations?—give details;

(i) the nature and cost of any alterations, additions or improvements made or to be made by the occupier as a condition of
his current tenancy;

(j) whether the tenancy is weekly, monthly, quarterly, yearly, or
for a term of years;

(k) details of the lease or agreement including: date of commence-
ment and term; conditions for termination; special conditions
(give details); payment of any premium; date and cost of any
assignment; date and details of any renewal of the lease,
following a surrender of a previous lease; details of any fixing
of the rent under landlord and tenant legislation;

(l) details of any subletting.

11.30 The form must be signed and dated and an indication given as
to the capacity in which the form is completed, ie whether it is the
owner, occupier or lessee who has submitted the information.

11.31 The return is to be delivered to the valuation officer within
twenty-one days after the date of service of the notice (s 82(3)). Failure
to do so without reasonable excuse renders the person on whom the
notice was served liable to a fine and further penalty if the failure
continues.

11.32 No form for the notice was prescribed under the GRA 1967;
however, the valuation office sends out a standard form (see Appendix
4, item 10). Section 82 rent returns can also be used in 'valuation
proceedings' (see 12.10 and 12.81–5).

Preparation of the list

11.33 It is the duty of the *valuation officer* to prepare a new valuation
list for the rating area at the times and in the form referred to above.

The omission from a new valuation list of any matter required by law to be included does not render the list invalid.

11.34   The valuation officer (and any person authorised by him) has power to enter on, survey and value any hereditament in the area for which the valuation officer acts. At least twenty-four hours' notice in writing must be given and the hour of entry and survey must be reasonable.

11.35   The valuation officer must sign and deposit the valuation list at the offices of the rating authority by the end of December for it to come into force the following April.

11.36   The rating authority immediately gives notice of the list and of the rights of persons to inspect and to make proposals for altering it. There is no right to object to the list before it takes effect, but after it does so, it can be altered by the making of a proposal (see Chapter 12).

11.37   After transmitting the list to the rating authority, but before it comes into force in April, the valuation officer has power to make alterations necessitated 'by reason of a material change of circumstances' (defined in s 68(4) as including the coming into occupation of a newly constructed hereditament or one that has been unoccupied on account of structural alterations, and events relating either to physical occurrences or changes in occupation affecting the basis of valuation). These 'alterations' are usually grouped separately within the body of the valuation list.

Inspection of the list

11.38   General provisions as to inspection are contained in s 108 and are applicable not only to a new List but to any valuation list. The right of inspection extends to notices of appeal, objections, proposals, and minutes of the proceedings of any rating authority and local valuation court.

11.39   On receiving the valuation list from the valuation officer, the rating authority deposits it at its offices and thereafter gives effect to any proper directions for alterations given to it by the valuation officer.

11.40   If, in the course of the exercise of its functions, any information comes to the notice of any local authority which leads it to suppose that the valuation list needs alteration, it is the duty of the authority to inform the valuation officer.

Proposals to alter the list within the first six months of it taking effect

11.41 Where the assessment of any hereditament in the new list exceeds the previous assessment although the hereditament has not been altered, if a proposal for a reduction is served within the first six months of the list taking effect, the amount of rates recoverable is limited to the amount levied in the previous year plus half the difference between that amount and the full rates otherwise recoverable, until the proposal is settled (s 8(1)). Under the 1980 Act, the Secretary of State has power to vary the proportion of rates withheld.

Checklist

11.42 The valuation officer is responsible for preparation, maintenance and alteration of the list. (Valuation officers are appointed by the Commissioners of Inland Revenue.)

11.43 The rating authority keeps the list and gives effect to directions from the valuation officer and informs him if the list needs altering. The list is available for public inspection.

11.44 The requirement for quinquennial revaluations is postponed and the Secretary of State will require new lists to come into force as and when specified by order (approved by Parliament).

11.45 On revaluation, a gross value is required only for 'domestic hereditaments'. Net annual value is required to be calculated directly for all other hereditaments. A revaluation is to be carried out for specified hereditaments only, with the 1973 rateable values of unspecified hereditaments either inserted into the new list or 'adjusted' prior to insertion. The Secretary of State has power to fix an antecedent valuation date prior to the date on which the list takes effect, at which date all values are to be correct.

11.46 The list must be in the form prescribed, covering each rating area. Except for agricultural, rail, canal, sewer and land drainage hereditaments, all hereditaments are entered in the list.

11.47 Returns (s 82) may be demanded from occupiers etc giving rental etc details in order to calculate net annual value in preparing a new list. The valuation officer has a right of entry to inspect and value all hereditaments.

11.48 The list must be signed and deposited with the rating authority at the end of December prior to the April when it comes into force. Proposals are allowed to alter the list only after it comes into force.

11.49 Provided a proposal is made to reduce the assessment within six months of the list coming into force, the rating authority can only levy half the increase in rates due until the proposal is settled.

Chapter 12

Proposals and appeals

Synopsis

12.1 Entries in the valuation list are altered by means of a 'Proposal to alter the valuation list'.

12.2 Anyone may make a proposal, as long as they are 'aggrieved' by the existing state of the list.

12.3 The valuation officer (who cannot be 'aggrieved') may make a proposal to ensure that the list is correct.

12.4 Proposals made by 'aggrieved persons' ('AP proposals') follow a defined and strict procedure. Valuation officer's proposals ('VO proposals') follow a different procedure. The legality of the proposal depends on the statutory procedures being adhered to.

12.5 The court of first instance is the local valuation court, an informal court which decides rating assessments and other connected matters.

12.6 Appeal from the local valuation court is to the Lands Tribunal and thence, on a point of law only, to the Court of Appeal.

Proposals to alter the valuation list

12.7 The way in which entries in the valuation list are altered is by a *'Proposal to alter the valuation list'*.

12.8 A *person who is aggrieved* may make a proposal for the alteration of the valuation list under certain specified grounds (see 12.13) (s 69(1)).

12.9 The *valuation officer* may at any time make a proposal for any alteration of a valuation list (s 69(2)) in order to comply with his duty to ensure that the valuation list is correct.

12.10 In deciding whether to make or object to a proposal, the valuation officer may require the completion of a rent return (s 82(2)) as though he were compiling a valuation list on revaluation (see 11.27–32).

12.11   A *rating authority* has specific power (s 69(3)) to make a proposal for the insertion of a new hereditament in the list, provided it does so within twenty-eight days after written notice from the valuation officer that he does not intend to make such a proposal himself. This is the only time when someone other than the valuation officer can propose the entry of a hereditament into the list for the first time (see 6.49).

Aggrieved persons

12.12   The right to make a proposal under s 69(1) is given to 'any person (including a rating authority) who is aggrieved'. This will include, as well as occupiers, owners rated under ss 55 and 56 (see 6.9–26), owners of unoccupied property and houses adapted for occupation in parts which are assessed as one hereditament (see 6.27–35).

12.13   Section 69(1) specifies the following grounds on which a proposal may be made by an aggrieved person:

(a) the inclusion of any hereditament in the valuation list;

(b) the value ascribed in the valuation list to a hereditament, or any other statement made or omitted to be made in the list with respect to a hereditament;

(c) in the case of a house or a portion of a building which is a 'house adapted for occupation in parts', the valuation in the list of that building or portion as a single hereditament.

12.14   The most common ground for grievance is that a hereditament has been overvalued.

12.15   Only the valuation officer (or exceptionally the rating authority) may make a proposal to insert a new hereditament in the list (s 69(3) and Scheds 1 and 6(1) and (2)).

Form of proposal

12.16   Section 69(5) requires that every proposal must be made *in writing*, specifying the *grounds* on which the proposed alteration is supported and complying with any regulations made. The Valuation List (Proposals for Alteration) Regulations 1974 contain a form for the making of proposals all of which must be 'in a form substantially to the like effect' (see Appendix 4, items 1–3).

12.17 The proposal must be signed either by the maker personally or a duly authorised agent. A proposal is not invalid because the address of the hereditament to which it refers is not exact, so long as it adequately identifies the hereditament.

12.18 The date of the proposal fixes the nature of the property, the state of the locality etc for the purposes of the valuation (bearing in mind tone of the list). The proposal should, therefore, be dated.

12.19 If a proposal is made by an aggrieved person, that person must show that he was *aggrieved at the date of the proposal*.

12.20 One proposal may be made relating to several hereditaments provided they are all in the same list, and either owned or occupied by the same person or comprised in the same building.

12.21 Every proposal must be *served on the valuation officer* (except where the valuation officer makes the proposal).

12.22 Because the procedures vary depending on whether the proposal is made by an aggrieved person (AP proposal) or by the valuation officer (VO proposal), the procedures will be treated separately.

Aggrieved person's proposal (AP proposal)

(See also 12.101 and Appendix 4, item 1.)

12.23 An aggrieved person's proposal *must be served on the valuation officer* for the area in which the hereditament is located.

12.24 Within twenty-eight days of the date on which it is served, the valuation officer will *serve a copy of the proposal* on the *occupier* of the hereditament to which it relates, the *rating authority* and any *rated owner* (rated under ss 55 and 56), unless any one of these is the maker of the proposal (s 70(1)).

12.25 Each of these persons (the occupier, the rating authority and rated owner), together with an owner not rated, is entitled to serve on the valuation officer a written *notice of objection* to the proposal within twenty-eight days of receipt of the proposal.

12.26 The *valuation officer may also object* to the proposal, but he has three months within which to do so (see Appendix 4, item 4 for a copy of a letter accompanying the valuation officer's objection).

12.27 If *no objections* are received within the time limit or if all objections are withdrawn unconditionally, the proposal is allowed to take effect, ie whatever alteration to the valuation list is proposed is actually implemented (and the proposal is called 'well founded').

12.28 If *objections are not withdrawn* unconditionally, one of three things must happen:

(a) either the *proposal is withdrawn* as a result of the objections, in which case no further action is taken; or

(b) a mutually acceptable *agreement* is negotiated (see 12.37–8), in which case it is the assessment resulting from the agreement which is entered into the valuation list; or

(c) if none of these events occurs, the *maker of the proposal is deemed to have appealed* against the objection to the *local valuation court*.

12.29 For the appeal to take place, the maker of the proposal need do nothing. His failure to withdraw his proposal is taken to be an indication of his desire to appeal. The appeal takes effect fourteen days after a valuation officer's objection or four months from the date of service of the proposal on the valuation officer, after an objection by another.

12.30 The procedure from this point is the same as that following a valuation officer's proposal (see 12.39 and 12.101).

Valuation officer's proposal (VO proposal)

(*GRA 1967, s 70(1)*—see 12.102 and Appendix 4, items 2 and 3.)

12.31 A copy of the *valuation officer's proposal* must be served within seven days on the occupier, the rating authority and any rated owner (under ss 55 and 56).

12.32 These persons, together with an owner not rated, have twenty-eight days within which to serve a written *notice of objection* on the valuation officer.

12.33 If *no objections* are received or if all objections are unconditionally withdrawn, the proposal is allowed to take effect as 'well founded'.

12.34 If *objections are not withdrawn* unconditionally, one of three things must happen:

(a) either the *proposal is withdrawn* as a result of the objections, in which case no further action is taken; or

(b) a mutually acceptable *agreement* is negotiated (see 12.37–8), in which case it is the assessment resulting from the agreement which is entered into the valuation list; or

(c) if none of these events occurs, the *valuation officer is deemed to have appealed* against the objection to the *local valuation court*.

12.35 As with the procedure for an aggrieved person's proposal, it is the valuation officer's failure to withdraw his proposal which is taken as indicating his desire to appeal.

12.36 However, unlike the aggrieved person's proposal, this appeal always takes place four months after the date of the proposal.

Agreement

12.37 Following negotiation, an agreement can be reached between the maker of the proposal and the objector and, provided all parties can agree, that agreed assessment may be entered into the valuation list (see Appendix 4, item 5 for agreement forms).

12.38 In at least one capacity the following must be a party to the agreement: the maker of the proposal, the objector, the valuation officer, the occupier, the rated owner, and the rating authority (although the rating authority must inform the valuation officer of its intention to be a party to any such agreement, unless it is also one of the previously mentioned parties).

Appeals

12.39 The appeal by the maker of the proposal (whether aggrieved person or valuation officer) takes the form of the valuation officer *sending copies of all relevant documents to the clerk* of the local valuation panel.

12.40 There is no requirement on the maker of the proposal to do anything for the appeal to be made, except to have failed to withdraw his proposal (see Appendix 4, item 6 for the valuation officer's explanation of procedure, including appeals).

Alterations to the valuation list without proposal

12.41 At any time the valuation officer may direct the rating authority to alter the list to correct any *clerical* or *arithmetical error* (eg totals).

12.42 The valuation officer may, if requested by the rating authority and satisfied that a hereditament has *ceased to exist*, cause that hereditament to be deleted from the list without a proposal.

Appeal to the local valuation court

12.43 As mentioned in 12.39, the appeal (whether AP or VO) procedure commences with the valuation officer sending copies of all relevant documents to the clerk of the *local valuation panel.*

12.44 The panel provides the members of the *local valuation court*, and appeals are heard by the chairman (or a deputy) and two other members of the panel (although any two may hear the appeal if all parties agree).

12.45 It is the chairman's duty to ensure that local valuation courts are convened as often as necessary to hear and determine appeals.

12.46 The local valuation court must *sit in public* unless, on application from one of the parties to the appeal, the court is satisfied that the parties' interests would be prejudicially affected by a public hearing.

12.47 The decisions as to *the order of listing of appeals* for hearing and which appeals are to be heard by the same court, rest with the local valuation panel. The panel generally takes account of the following:

(a) appeals may be concerned with a common factor of valuation, eg similar shops in the same shopping centre;

(b) an early determination of an issue by the court can lead to subsequent settlement out of court of appeals based on similar issues;

(c) it may be important to have all appeals relating to a particular problem heard in sequence by the same members;

(d) the decision of a court on a matter of law or valuation in one case may have a direct bearing on similar issues in other appeals in the same panel area;

(e) there may be reasons why certain appeals should be listed for an early hearing (eg where the state of the hereditament or locality at the date of valuation is about to undergo a fundamental change);

(f) there may also be reasons why certain appeals should be heard at a later date (eg where a hereditament is subject to building alterations which have reached an intermediate stage at the date of valuation);

(g) where it is likely to be argued that properties might be valued on 'throughput' or accounts, it may be advisable to postpone the hearing until the appropriate year's results are known;

(h) following revaluation there is a need to determine appeals on all types of property and not, for example, to concentrate on appeals on residential hereditaments (usually the largest in number).

12.48 Experience has shown that generally it is not helpful to list appeals for hearing together:

(a) in order of receipt;
(b) in respect of various types of property in the same locality;
(c) where the same agent is acting for the ratepayers.

Negotiations between the parties

12.49 Because a substantial number of proposals are settled at the appeal stage without the need for a hearing by the court, it is important that discussions with the valuation officer (who can give effect to contentions) and other parties should take place well in advance of the court hearing.

12.50 Many proposals submitted by aggrieved persons do not disclose the assessment contended for, and it is necessary that the valuation officer be made aware of the proposed assessment at an early stage. (Such a proposal can never be allowed as 'well founded'.)

12.51 The parties should agree all factual matters (especially areas) and be prepared to exchange valuations and evidence of rents and assessments.

12.52 Where there is a dispute affecting several ratepayers, such as the general basis of assessment on a particular type of hereditament, it may be helpful if the valuation officer and valuers concerned meet to discuss the general problem before individual meetings are arranged to discuss the individual hereditaments. Normally the valuation officer will only discuss a case with the ratepayer or agent concerned unless, on representation, he considers an alternative approach preferable.

12.53 All parties to negotiations should inform the clerk to the panel at an early stage if it is evident that certain appeals could benefit from being listed for the same court, and indicate the likely time required for hearing.

12.54 When appeals have been listed for hearing, parties should keep the clerk to the panel informed of the progress of negotiations and the likelihood of a pre-court settlement.

Notice of hearing

12.55 Under reg 4(1) of the Rating Appeals (Local Valuation Courts) Regulations 1956:

> The clerk shall give not less than 14 days' notice of the date, time and place fixed for the hearing of an appeal to the appellant and to every person who has served, and has not unconditionally withdrawn, a notice of objection to the proposal.

12.56 It is generally accepted that this minimum notice is neither practical nor appropriate. Often twenty-eight days' notice is given in the case of appeals on domestic hereditaments, and sometimes two months for appeals on commercial and industrial premises.

12.57 Notices of hearing should be sent to all parties simultaneously.

12.58 Because parties not present at a hearing have *no right of appeal* to the Lands Tribunal against a decision of the court, is important that any reasonable application for postponement is dealt with sympathetically.

12.59 The decision to grant a postponement rests with the chairman of the court who, in consultation with the clerk, may allow a postponement in such circumstances as:

   (a) any party or representative unable to appear due to an engagement in another local valuation court or a higher court, absence on holiday or special business, or illness;

   (b) the time allowed for the hearing is considered insufficient and it would be more appropriate to allocate another day or days for the hearing;

   (c) adjournment pending the decision in another case where similar issues are involved;

   (d) where agreement has been reached by two or more parties shortly before the hearing and there is insufficient time for all parties to complete the agreement form procedure. In this case, the court should be satisfied that all parties are prepared to sign the agreement forms, otherwise the case should be heard as usual.

12.60 Applications for adjournments should be made as early as possible to the clerk of the court, and the clerk kept informed of all developments or likely developments.

Court procedure

12.61   The following persons are entitled to appear in at least one of the following capacities, to be heard as parties to the appeal, and to call and examine witnesses:

(a) the maker of the proposal, being the appellant;
(b) the valuation officer;
(c) the occupier;
(d) the owner;
(e) the rating authority;
(f) the maker of the objection, being the objector or respondent.

12.62   Identification of the parties present will include members of the press, if any attend (it is a public hearing unless accounts are being presented in evidence and their presentation before the public is likely to be prejudicial to the case).

12.63   If a party to the hearing fails to appear, having satisfied itself that the required notices have been given, the court may proceed on the assumption that that party does not desire to be heard.

12.64   *The appellant normally opens the proceedings*, although where the appellant is an unrepresented ratepayer the valuation officer may be asked to present his case first. It is for the court to decide, with the appellant's agreement.

12.65   Apart from this, *it is for the court to determine the procedure* which may be varied depending on the circumstances.

12.66   The *normal practice* is as follows.

(a) The appellant states his case. The onus of proof is on the appellant.
(b) The appellant may call witnesses who may be cross-examined by any party.
(c) The appellant may be cross-examined on his evidence.
(d) The objector states the grounds for his objection.
(e) The objector may call witnesses who may be cross-examined by any party.
(f) The objector may be cross-examined on his evidence.
(g) The objector concludes his case, without introducing any new evidence. If new evidence is introduced, other parties must be given the opportunity to question the objector and reply. He must state his contention (ie the rating assessment he is asking the court to determine).
(h) The appellant makes his final submission but must not introduce any new evidence. The appellant must state his conten-

tion. (Despite the lack of a fixed procedure at local valuation court, the appellant is always allowed the last word!)

12.67 The *rating authority* may be represented by its clerk or other duly appointed representative. The rating authority's representative may appear in respect of the rating authority's properties or on behalf of ratepayers as a whole. He may support any other parties or present a separate case. As a party to the appeal, he is entitled to cross-examine any witnesses. Unless the rating authority is the appellant or the objector, the case for the rating authority is normally presented after that of the other parties.

12.68 Evidence may be taken on oath although this is not common practice.

12.69 The court may wish to inspect the appeal hereditament or may be asked to do so. It is for the court to decide whether an inspection is necessary and, if so, it will usually take place after the evidence has been heard, with either all or none of the parties present.

12.70 Local valuation courts are governed by the Tribunals and Inquiries Act 1971 under which it is the duty of the court, if requested, on or before the giving of a decision to furnish a statement, either written or oral, of the *reasons* for the decision.

12.71 A copy of *the decision* is sent to every party to the appeal and will include a statement as to the right of appeal to the Lands Tribunal against the decision.

12.72 Decisions of the local valuation court must be recorded and be open to public inspection at all reasonable times, as are the minutes of a local valuation court hearing.

12.73 A local valuation court hearing will involve no court costs unless the parties appoint professional advisers, in which case each party will be responsible for the fees of such advisers or representatives. Any representatives should be given written authority to act for a party.

12.74 The local valuation court's *jurisdiction is limited*, in that if a proposal is made for an increase in the assessment it cannot decide to decrease the assessment and vice versa (although a new proposal may be made). If the proposal is to enter a new assessment in the list, the local valuation court has no power to determine a figure higher than that proposed.

12.75 'Ratepayers are assured of every reasonable consideration by the court and assistance will be given to them in submitting relevant facts. Due allowance will be made for those who may be unfamiliar with court procedure.' (*Rating Appeals to Local Valuation Court in England and Wales* (LVP/GN/1).)

12.76 The decision of the court is to be that of the majority, in writing signed by the person acting as chairman at the meeting of the court, and must embody any directions of the court as to the amendment of the valuation list.

Effect of court's decision

12.77 The valuation officer must cause to be made in the valuation list such alterations as are necessary to give effect to the decision of the court, that is to say he must give directions to the rating authority which must comply with them.

Directions

12.78 The decisions of the local valuation court and any proposals allowed as 'well founded' are entered into the valuation list. This is done by the valuation officer who issues 'directions' to the rating authority on the alteration to be made. Any existing entry is deleted and a reference number prefaced with the letter D (for direction) will indicate the location (page and line) of the new entry (see 11.17).

Date of alteration in pursuance of proposals

12.79 Any alteration following a proposal is back-dated to the ***beginning of the rate period*** during which it was served, eg a proposal served 1 July 1987 is effective from 1 April 1987.

12.80 This general rule is subject to the following exceptions, in which cases the proposal takes effect from ***the date of the event*** which gives rise it:

  (a) the bringing into occupation of a hereditament, previously unoccupied or non-existent;
  (b) value altered by structural alterations;
  (c) an event whereby a hereditament becomes or ceases to be rated;
  (d) any property previously rated as a single hereditament becoming liable to be rated in parts and vice versa;
  (e) any changes in the extent to which railway or canal premises are occupied for non-rateable purposes.

Use of rent returns

12.81 Section 82 rent returns contain the particulars provided by an occupier etc for the valuation officer to compile the list, or to decide whether or not to make or object to a proposal (see 11.27–32, 12.10 and Appendix 4, item 10). Such returns are not available for public inspection but are used in 'valuation proceedings' as evidence of fact.

12.82 Before such returns may be used by the valuation officer, he must give not less than fourteen days' notice to the maker of the proposal and to every objector whose objection is still outstanding. The notice must specify the returns to be used and the hereditaments to which they relate, and give the name of person making the return. The valuation officer must give persons receiving the notice the opportunity to inspect and take extracts from these returns.

12.83 A person who receives notice of the use of s 82 returns may serve a notice on the valuation officer specifying hereditaments which are comparable in character and relevant to the case, and require the valuation officer to permit him to inspect and take extracts from any returns which relate to the hereditaments he has specified. The valuation officer is also required to produce these at the hearing. The number of hereditaments a person may specify must not exceed the number specified by the valuation officer in his original notice.

12.84 Once the valuation officer gives notice of his intention to use rent returns, any other party may give notice of an intention to use them; but if the valuation officer chooses not to rely on s 82 evidence, no one else can do so.

12.85 Section 82 rent returns contain such particulars as may reasonably be required for the purpose of enabling the valuation officer to decide whether or not to make or, as the case may be, object to the proposal or to enable him to compile the valuation list (s 82(1)–(2)). Accordingly, where a valuation officer sought to introduce evidence of a rent return obtained by him for the purposes of presenting his case, the Lands Tribunal held that such evidence was inadmissible (*Lach* v *Williamson (VO)* (1957)). However, in *Smith* v *Moore (VO)* (1972), the Lands Tribunal held that returns which had been obtained by the valuation officer in the normal course of assembling information for the purpose of preparing a new valuation list were admissible as evidence.

Arbitration

12.86 Instead of going before a local valuation court by way of appeal against an objection to a proposal, the persons who would have been entitled to appear and be heard before such a court may, in writing, agree to refer to arbitration any matter which would otherwise have come before that court for hearing or determination (s 78(1)).

12.87 The Arbitration Act 1950 is to apply to any such arbitration (s 78(2)), and the award can include any directions which might have been given by the local valuation court. The valuation officer is bound to treat them as he would a court decision (s 78(3)). If, however, the parties agree to appoint the Lands Tribunal as arbitrator (s 1(5) of the Lands Tribunal Act 1949), the Arbitration Act is to apply only in so far as it is applied by the Lands Tribunal Rules 1975 (Lands Tribunal Rules 1975, r 38).

12.88 This power can be a convenient one for the cases which the parties intend from the beginning to take before the tribunal, since it saves both the time and the expense of a hearing before the local valuation court.

Appeal to the Lands Tribunal

12.89 Any party actually present at a local valuation court hearing has the right to appeal against that court's decision to the Lands Tribunal within twenty-eight days (s 77).

12.90 It is therefore necessary for a case to have been heard at local valuation court level and for the appellant to have been present and heard at that court before an appeal can be made to the Lands Tribunal. Presence at court may, of course, be by representative.

12.91 Appearance at the Lands Tribunal will involve costs, awarded at its discretion.

12.92 A decision by the Lands Tribunal is final, save that an appeal *on a point of law* lies to the Court of Appeal, and thence to the House of Lords. However, in either case, if the decision on the legal point involves a reconsideration of the valuation, the case is referred back to the Lands Tribunal, which is the highest court on the valuation of land.

Checklist

12.93 The valuation officer and any 'aggrieved person' can make a proposal to alter the valuation list (see 12.101 and 102 for procedures).

12.94 Valuation officers may require s 82 rent returns before deciding to make or object to a proposal. An aggrieved person's proposal may only be made on specified grounds.

12.95   There is no set form for the proposal, but date of proposal is the valuation date (bear in mind tone of the list). Valuation officers may alter lists without a proposal to correct arithmetical errors and to delete a non-existent hereditament.

12.96   The local valuation court is the court of first instance; an informal court with informal procedures, where no costs are awarded unless a professional representative is employed. The clerk notifies all parties of the hearing. The court gives reasons for decisions if asked, and has a limited jurisdiction.

12.97   Proposals are effective as at the beginning of the rate period during which served, except where a hereditament comes into or goes out of occupation and structural alterations have taken place etc.

12.98   The list is altered by directions given to a rating authority from the valuation officer.

12.99   As an alternative to a local valuation court, cases may be heard by arbitration.

12.100   Appeals from a local valuation court are to the Lands Tribunal but only by a party present at the local valuation court hearing. From the Lands Tribunal, appeal on a point of law only is allowed to the Court of Appeal and thence to the House of Lords.

12.101   Table 12.101 shows the procedure followed in an aggrieved person's proposal.

Table 12.101   Aggrieved person's proposal procedure (GRA 1967, Part V)

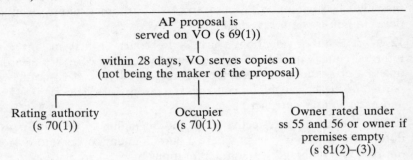

AP proposal is
served on VO (s 69(1))

within 28 days, VO serves copies on
(not being the maker of the proposal)

| Rating authority (s 70(1)) | Occupier (s 70(1)) | Owner rated under ss 55 and 56 or owner if premises empty (s 81(2)–(3)) |

These persons together with an owner not rated may serve notice of objection on the valuation officer within 28 days of receipt of the copy of the proposal (s 70(2)). Valuation officer may object within 3 months of receipt of proposal (s 74(1))

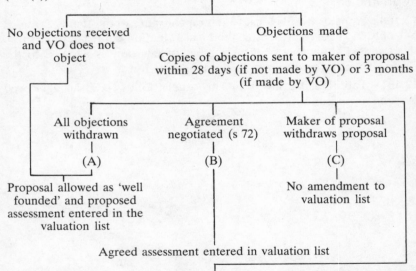

No objections received and VO does not object

Objections made

Copies of objections sent to maker of proposal within 28 days (if not made by VO) or 3 months (if made by VO)

All objections withdrawn	Agreement negotiated (s 72)	Maker of proposal withdraws proposal
(A)	(B)	(C)
Proposal allowed as 'well founded' and proposed assessment entered in the valuation list		No amendment to valuation list

Agreed assessment entered in valuation list

If proposal not settled, within 14 days of notice of VO's objection or 4 months of receipt of proposal by VO, maker of proposal is deemed to have appealed to LVC against the objection (ss 73(1) and 74(1))

Copy of proposal and objections sent to local valuation panel (s 76(1)). Maker of proposal, objectors and rating authority informed (s 73(2)(*a*))

If still no settlement under (A), (B) or (C) above case heard by LVC (s 76(1))

LVC decision entered into valuation list

12.102 Table 12.102 shows the procedure for a valuation officer's proposal.

Table 12.102 Valuation officer's proposal procedure (GRA 1967, Part V)

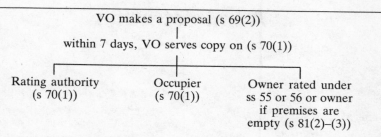

VO makes a proposal (s 69(2))

within 7 days, VO serves copy on (s 70(1))

| Rating authority (s 70(1)) | Occupier (s 70(1)) | Owner rated under ss 55 or 56 or owner if premises are empty (s 81(2)–(3)) |

These persons together with an owner not rated may serve notice of objection on VO within 28 days of date of service (s 70(2))

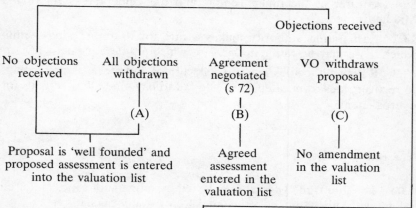

Objections received

| No objections received | All objections withdrawn | Agreement negotiated (s 72) | VO withdraws proposal |

(A)   (B)   (C)

| Proposal is 'well founded' and proposed assessment is entered into the valuation list | Agreed assessment entered in the valuation list | No amendment in the valuation list |

If proposal not settled, VO is deemed to appeal to LVC within 4 months of date of making proposal

Copy of proposal and objections sent to clerk to LVC (s 73(1), (2)(*b*)). Objectors and rating authority informed (s 73(2)(*a*))

If still no settlement under (A), (B) or (C) case heard by LVC (s 76(1))

LVC decision entered in the valuation list

Chapter 13

Administration

General

13.1 Rates are administered by rating authorities, ie district councils, borough councils, the Common Council of the City of London, the Sub-Treasurer of the Inner Temple and the Under-Treasurer of the Middle Temple.

13.2 Each rating authority makes a rate for its rating area, within which there may be rating districts-for which a different rate is levied.

13.3 Rating authorities levy and collect rates, initiate legal proceedings to recover rates from ratepayers who fail to pay, and allow refunds for overpayment.

The rate

13.4 The rate is the *general rate*, levied by rating authorities and used (along with other sources of income) to provide local services.

13.5 The rate must make up any shortfall between other sources of income and the estimated expenditure required for the rate period.

13.6 The money raised by the rating authority must include amounts payable to other authorities which have precepted on the rating authority, ie money required in rates for county and parish or community councils.

13.7 The rate must be levied at a *uniform rate in the pound* throughout the rating area. However, where there is for example a parish council responsible for part of a rating area, the rate in the pound for the area covered by the parish council will be increased for the parish council's precept. To that extent *differential rating* may occur.

13.8 The rate in the pound applied to domestic hereditaments and mixed hereditaments is reduced by the prescribed amount (see 5.95–5.104).

13.9 A rate is made by resolution of the rating authority by reference to the valuation list in force at the time or, if a new valuation list is to take effect, by reference to that new valuation list.

13.10 The rate is made in respect of a period commencing immediately after the expiration of the period of the preceding rate (s 3(3)), so that there is never an interval without a current general rate. The length of the period of the rate is a complete financial year (Local Government Finance Act 1982).

13.11 A ratepayer may require the rating authority to provide him with a statement of rates payable or paid in respect of the property he occupies.

13.12 The accounts of the rating authority are subject to the scrutiny of the district auditor, and must contain prescribed information (Rate Account (Amendment) Regulations 1966).

Appeals against the rate

13.13 No appeal against the rate exists if a remedy may be obtained by means of a proposal for the alteration of the current valuation list or an objection to such a proposal or appeal against such an objection (s 7).

13.14 Appeals against the rate are made to the Crown Court by any person who:

(a) is aggrieved by the rate; or
(b) has any material objection to the inclusion or exclusion of any person in or from, or to the amount charged to any person in, any rate; or
(c) is aggrieved by any neglect, act or thing done or omitted by the rating authority.

13.15 Examples of grounds of appeal against the rate are that the rate has not been made in the manner required by statute, that the rate was not duly published, or that the rate was not made according to the rateable values shown in the valuation list in force.

13.16 There is a right of appeal to the High Court from the decision of the Crown Court.

Payment of rates

(*GRA 1967, s 10*)

13.17   Rates are an occupiers' tax. The occupier is rateable in respect of the property he occupies (subject, of course, to the statutory provisions for rating owners under certain circumstances—see Chapter 6).

13.18   Rates are levied on persons who occupy property at the beginning and during the course of the rate period (1 April to 31 March).

13.19   Initially, it is the person in occupation at the beginning of the rate period who is liable for rates during the whole period. However, if there is a change of occupier during the rate period, rates are demanded from the second occupier for his period of occupation and refunded to the first occupier for his period of non-occupation.

13.20   The rating authorities must send to all ratepayers a demand containing:

(a) the situation and description of the hereditament;
(b) the rateable value;
(c) the rate in the pound and the rate period;
(d) the amount in the pound which is levied by each authority within each rating area; this will include all precepts by county and parish or community councils and supplementary rate;
(e) any other information which is required by the Rate Demand Rules 1981.

13.21   Rates are payable in one lump sum at the beginning of the rate period; however, there is a right under certain circumstances to pay rates *by instalments*.

13.22   Rates may be paid in instalments by occupiers of all classes of property purely at the discretion of the rating authority.

13.23   There is a statutory right to pay rates in ten instalments if an occupier is liable for rates on a 'domestic hereditament' or for any other hereditament with a rateable value exceeding £100 and not exceeding £2,000 (£5,000 in Greater London) (s 50 and Sched 10 of the GRA 1967, as amended).

13.24   There is no statutory right to pay rates by instalments for an owner who is compounded under ss 55 or 56 (see Chapter 6), or for a tenant of the rating authority who pays rates as part of his rent.

13.25   In addition, there may be a right to receive a discount for prompt payment (see 13.51–3).

Rate recovery

13.26 Since rates (like all taxes) are a creation of statute no common law remedies apply.

13.27 Indeed, statutory provisions must exist for all actions in relation to any tax; they cannot be assumed.

13.28 It is usual to recover unpaid rates by distraining on a ratepayer's goods and chattels, as provided by s 96.

13.29 On failing to pay rates which have been legally demanded, the rating authority may apply to a magistrates' court for a *distress warrant*.

13.30 There are grounds for resisting distress proceedings, such as the rate already having been paid, or that the person accused is not liable to pay the rates.

13.31 Where a person occupies only part of a hereditament he may be liable for the rates for the whole hereditament. This will occur when it is not clear from the description in the valuation list whether the ratepayer occupies all or only part of the property.

13.32 Thus if, for example, a property is described as 'shop, offices and premises' but the person from whom the rates are demanded occupies only the shop, that person cannot be required to pay rates on the whole hereditament.

13.33 The solution to the rating authority's problem is to make a proposal to reassess the property so that an entry in the list appears for the occupied shop on which rates can be levied.

13.34 However, if the property is described as 'shop' but the person from whom rates is demanded occupies only part of that shop, the information in the valuation list will not show that he is in occupation of part only of a hereditament. Under such circumstances the rating authority can require the occupier of part of the hereditament to pay rates on the whole.

13.35 Again, the solution is for the ratepayer to make a proposal to have the property reassessed, so that he pays rates only for the premises he occupies.

13.36 It is not possible to occupy part only of a purpose-built dwelling-house and pay rates for only part of the hereditament as described above, unless the remainder is rateably occupied by another and the two parts are capable of being defined and assessed as a hereditament (see Chapter 4 and *R* v *Aberystwyth* (1808)).

13.37 When issuing a distress warrant, defences which relate to incorrect procedures in compiling or maintaining the valuation list are irrelevant. The justices must accept the valuation list and its entries and not inquire whether the list is wrong.

13.38 If a valuation list is wrong or statutory procedures not observed, there is a remedy which the ratepayer should observe (such as making a proposal to alter the list).

13.39 A distress warrant cannot be withheld on the ground of hardship, although the rating authority may reduce or remit the payment of rates because of poverty (s 53, see 5.60–1).

13.40 An appeal against a magistrates' court decision is allowed to the High Court on a point of law only.

13.41 Distress is to be levied on a defaulter's goods and chattels found anywhere in England and Wales.

13.42 If the amount raised by the sale of such goods and chattels is insufficient to cover the debt, a *warrant for commital to prison* may be issued against the defaulter (ss 102 and 103).

13.43 Committal procedures will only be instigated where failure to pay results from wilful refusal or culpable neglect.

13.44 Following the term of imprisonment (not to exceed three months) it is usual for the debt to be written off by the rating authority.

13.45 Where a landlord is liable for rates and fails to pay, the rating authority may notify the tenant to pay his rent directly to the rating authority until the debt is paid (s 61). Should the occupier fail to do so, the rating authority may distrain on his goods and chattels as if he were directly liable for the rates (s 62).

13.46 Where an owner pays rates either under compulsory or voluntary compounding provisions, rates may be recovered from him as if he were an occupier (ie distress and committal procedures (GRA 1967, s 57) (see also 6.23–4).

13.47 However, where an owner agrees merely to collect rates from the occupier with the rent and to pay them to the rating authority, he is liable only for the proportion of rates that the total amount of rent and rates collected bears to the total amount of rent and rates due (s 56(5)—see also 6.20).

13.48 Where the property on which rates are due is a domestic hereditament and the ratepayer has a legal interest in the property, under s 107A of the 1967 Act (inserted by the 1980 Act) the ratepayer may agree that outstanding rates be secured by a mortgage on the hereditament in exchange for a declaration by the rating authority that it will not exercise its powers to proceed with recovering the arrears.

13.49 In the case of the *rating surcharge*—now suspended (see 6.53–8)—any unpaid rates (and surcharge) can be registered as a land charge, ie a debt on the ownership of the property, and are attached to the land until paid.

13.50 Where *property is unoccupied* and the rating authority attempts to recover unpaid rates (including the now suspended rating surcharge), this can be done by action for a simple contract debt (Sched 1 para 13 of the GRA 1967) in addition to the normal remedies.

Discounts

13.51 Under s 54 of the GRA 1967, discounts may be given by the rating authority to ratepayers who pay promptly.

13.52 This is a discretionary power to encourage ratepayers to pay, and thus to ensure an early flow of income to local authorities' funds.

13.53 Domestic ratepayers who pay by instalments are not entitled to a discount. But, under s 51, a domestic ratepayer who decides not to pay by instalments can receive a discount for prompt payment. Owners who pay rates under the compulsory or voluntary compounding provisions are also entitled to a discount (see 6.12 and 6.16).

Refunds

13.54 Under s 9, the *rating authority has discretionary power* to refund an overpayment of rates where:

  (a) the rateable value in the valuation list was excessive;
  (b) the ratepayer was entitled to an exemption or relief from rates which was not made;
  (c) the hereditament was unoccupied;
  (d) the person paying the rates was not liable for them; or
  (e) the rate was not levied in accordance with the list; and
  (f) the request is made within six years of the overpayment.

13.55 Where, for example, an assessment has been reduced because the assessment was excessive, a ratepayer may ask the rating authority to refund the additional rates paid to the date when the excessive valuation took effect.

13.56 If the rating authority is prepared to make a refund, a *valuation officer's certificate* is obtained stating the value of the hereditament as at the date from which the refund is requested and on which the rating authority will calculate the refund.

13.57 A certificate from the valuation officer (also called a s 9 certificate) is only required where the value in the list has been in question.

13.58 The rating authority's discretionary power to give a refund becomes mandatory where, for example, the court orders a refund (s 7(4)(*b*)), or where overpayment results from an error in administration.

13.59 Where, as the result of a proposal to alter the valuation list, the reduction in the assessment takes effect as from the date of the proposal or the beginning of the rate period in which the proposal was made, the rating authority must refund any excess rates paid since that date.

Bibliography

Barnfield, J O, Longden, G H and others, *Rating Law and Practice*, Rating and Valuation Association.

Emeny, R and Wilks, H, *Principles and Practice of Rating Valuation*, Estates Gazette.

Paying for Local Government, Cmnd 9714, HMSO.

Plimmer, F, *Zoning*, Polytechnic of Wales.

Royal Institution of Chartered Surveyors, *Practice Notes on Rating Appeals*, as reported in Chartered Surveyor, November 1979.

Sales, Harry (General Editor), *Encyclopaedia of Rating Law and Practice*, Sweet & Maxwell.

Sedgwick, J R E and Westbrook, R W, *The Valuation and Development of Petrol Filling Stations*, Estates Gazette.

Terminology (a periodically published series of articles in the Estates Gazette, first appearing 30 July 1983—267 EG 428).

Westbrook, R W, *The Valuation of Licensed Premises*, Estates Gazette.

Widdicombe, D, Eve, D T and Anderson, A, *Ryde on Rating*, Butterworths.

See also the references listed in Appendix 2.

History of rating

The Poor Relief Act 1601

Provision for the levying of a local tax at regular intervals over the whole country.
Appointment of Overseers of the Poor to:

(a) collect, spend and administer taxation;
(b) provide work for able-bodied unemployed, and give relief to those incapable of working;
(c) assess and levy a poor rate on every inhabitant and occupier to finance the above (no basis of assessment laid down).

Right of appeal to the quarter sessions.

Sir Anthony Earby's case (1633)

Parish poor rate could be levied only on property within that parish.
If rates are levied on an occupier, they can not also be levied on the landlord of the same property.

Poor Rate Exemption Act 1833

Exempted places of worship of denominations other than Church of England—not rated in practice under the 1601 Act.

Poor Law Amendment Act 1834

Administrative unit was reorganised into unions of parishes.
Responsibility for poor relief was transferred to the Board of Guardians of the Poor in each union.

Parochial Assessment Act 1836

First definition of 'net annual value'.

Poor Rate Exemption Act 1840

Abolished the taxation of stock-in-trade.
Abolished the liability of 'every inhabitant' within a parish to liability to rates.

Scientific Societies Act 1843

Scientific societies, ie those instituted for the purposes of science, literature or the fine arts exclusively, exempted from rates.

Union Assessment Committee Act 1862

Provided a definition of 'gross estimated rental'.
Provided for assessment committees to supervise assessments.
Required overseers to prepare and keep a valuation list.
Gave the right of objection to assessments.

Valuation (Metropolis) Act 1869

Separate gross value and rateable value definitions.
First scale for repair definitions.
Until 1963 London had a separate system of assessment and collection of rates from the remainder of England and Wales. The system was progressively reduced until, for the 1963 list, it was virtually the same as that of the rest of the country.

Rating Act 1874

Extended rateable property to all woodlands, sporting rights when severed from the occupation of land, and all mines.
Repealed so much of the 1601 Act as related to the taxation of an occupier of saleable woodlands.

Advertising Stations (Rating) Act 1889

Governed the rating of advertising stations.

Agricultural Rates Act 1896

Granted a 50 per cent relief from rates for agricultural land.

Agricultural Rates Act 1923

Granted a 75 per cent relief from rates for agricultural land.

Rating and Valuation Act 1925

New definitions of 'gross value', 'net annual value' and 'rateable value' to promote uniformity.
Abolition of overseers and a transfer of their functions to rating authorities.
Repeal of Union Assessment Acts.
Requirement for quinquennial revaluations.
Institution of the 'general rate'.
New system of appeals.
Rating of owners, where more convenient than rating occupiers.

Rating and Valuation (Apportionment) Act 1928

Defined industrial and freight-transport hereditaments.

Local Government Act 1929

Functions of unions of parishes transferred to county or county borough councils.
Complete exemption from rates for agricultural land and buildings.
Granted a 75 per cent relief from rates to industrial and freight-transport hereditaments.

Tithe Act 1936

Extinguished tithe rent charges and reduced the rating of tithes to a few tithes of a special nature.

Local Government Act 1948

Responsibility for the making, keeping and amending of the valuation list transferred to the Inland Revenue.
Introduction of a system of exchequer grants.

Introduction of local valuation courts as the courts of first instance, replacing assessment committees.

Provided for the rating of advertising rights when let out or reserved to anyone other than the occupier.

Laing (John) & Sons Ltd v *Kingswood Assessment Area Assessment Committee* (1949)

Recognition of the four essential ingredients of rateable occupation.

Valuation for Rating Act 1953

Introduced for the 1956 valuation lists, until 1963, a 1939 rental value basis for dwellinghouses.

Rating and Valuation (Miscellaneous Provisions) Act 1955

Replaced Poor Rate Exemption Act 1833.
    Granted relief from rates for charities, welfare structures and sewers.

Rating and Valuation Act 1957

Granted a one-fifth reduction in the assessments of commercial and business properties until 1963.

Local Government Act 1958

Reduced the relief from rates for industrial and freight-transport hereditaments to 50 per cent.

Rating and Valuation Act 1961

Abolished relief given to industrial and freight-transport hereditaments.
    Introduced a formula method of valuations for premises occupied by statutory undertakings etc.
    Enabled rating authorities to forgo rates on hereditaments for a short time.

Diplomatic Privileges Act 1964

Replaced common law immunity from payment of rates with statutory immunity.

Local Government Act 1966

Introduced discretionary power of the rating authority to collect rates on unoccupied buildings.
Reduced the rate in the pound for dwellinghouses.
Introduced statutory 'tone of the list' for proposals after 2 December 1965.
Introduced rebates for residential occupiers with low incomes.
Repealed so much of the 1601 Act as to leave only 'occupiers' liable for rates.
Abolished the rating of tithes.

General Rate Act 1967

Consolidated all prior current legislation.

General Rate Act 1970

Widened the scope of evidence which could be produced to justify the assessment of dwellinghouses in a new valuation list, to include the ratio between rent and gross value and to allow different dwelling types to be comparable.

Mines and Quarries (Valuation) Order 1971

Granted a 50 per cent reduction in rateable value from 1 April 1972 for mines and quarries, including those of the NCB.

Rating Act 1971

Exempted from rating 'factory farms' for the intensive raising of stock.

Local Government Act 1974

Minor structural alterations to dwellinghouses not assessable until revaluation.
New rebate scheme for occupiers of dwellinghouses.
Amendment to powers of rating authorities to rate unoccupied properties (abolition of the seven-year rule).
Introduction of the penal surcharge on unoccupied commercial buildings, levied on the owner.

Layfield Report on Local Government Finance (published May 1976)

Recommendations included:

(a) capital value rating for domestic properties;

(b) rental value retained for non-domestic properties;
(c) regular and frequent (three-yearly) revaluations;
(d) speeding up of appeals to local valuation courts;
(e) appeal to Lands Tribunal only on points of law, precedent and complex cases.

Rating (Caravan Sites) Act 1976

Valuation officer's discretion to rate leisure caravans on site separately, or to assess the whole site as one hereditament.

Rating (Charity Shops) Act 1976

Amended s 40 of the GRA 1967, so that charity shops are exempt.

Rating (Disabled Persons) Act 1978

Repealed s 45 of the GRA 1967.
   Relief is given by the rating authority in rate rebates on dwellings adapted for disabled persons and on institutions for the disabled.

Valuation Lists (Postponement) Order 1978

Postponed the requirement for new valuation lists for another year (postponed annually until 1980) to allow consideration to be given to alter the present rating system.

Local Government Planning and Land Act 1980

Abolishes requirement for quinquennial revaluations. Future revaluations ordered by Secretary of State, who may specify hereditaments to be revalued and allow adjustment of assessments of hereditaments not revalued.
   On next revaluation, all hereditaments except 'domestic hereditaments' will be valued to net annual value direct.
   On next revaluation, valuations may be made as at a specified time, subject to certain assumptions regarding 'relevant factors'.
   Fish farms not rated.
   Extension of domestic rate relief to hereditaments which include some residential accommodation.
   Extension of right to pay rates by instalments to occupiers of non-domestic hereditaments.

Secretary of State may vary proportion of rates withheld during first year of a list pending settlement of a proposal to alter that list.

Rating authority may vary percentage reductions given to owners who are rated in place of the occupier (ss 55 and 56 of the GRA 1967).

Secretary of State may direct that s 17A of the GRA 1967 (surcharge provisions) shall cease to have effect and, having done so, may reintroduce those provisions by order.

Secretary of State may vary three- (or six-) month period of non-occupation before rates paid on unoccupied newly built premises.

Non-domestic hereditaments etc in an enterprise zone are exempt rates.

Rating Surcharge (Suspension) Order 1980

Provisions of s 17A of the GRA 1967 (introduced by Local Government Act 1974) ceased to have effect as from 1 April 1981. (Note the provisions are not abolished, only suspended.)

Alternative to Domestic Rates (published December 1981)

Government Green Paper offering 'for public discussion the results of a review by the government of possible local revenue'.

Local Government Finance Act 1982

Abolished supplementary rates and supplementary precepts.
  Required rates and precepts to be made for complete financial years.
  Provided for the making of substituted rates and substituted precepts.
  Regulations for challenging the validity of the rate and precepts.
  Relief from rates for enterprise zones—additional provisions.
  New auditing provisions.

Social Security and Housing Benefits Act 1982

Abolishes previous rate rebate scheme (under GRA 1967 and Local Government Act 1974).

New scheme grants rate rebates along with rent rebates and rent allowances as housing benefits.

Rates—Proposals for Rate Limitation and Reform of the Rating System (published August 1983)

Government White Paper proposing reform of the rating system and 'rate-capping' of individual local authorities together with a general power to limit rate increases for all authorities.

Rating (Exemption of Unoccupied Industrial Hereditaments) Regulations 1984

Amends Sched 1 of the GRA 1967 in that from 1 April 1984 local authorities' powers to levy rates on empty industrial property are suspended.

Rates Act 1984

Introduced 'rate-capping', ie selective and general limitation of rates and precepts.

Duty on rating authorities to consult industrial and commercial ratepayers in fixing rate in the pound.

Duty to inform ratepayers of proposed expenditure and any increase/decrease in rates.

Exempts non-domestic hereditaments not in active use.

Discretion of valuation officer to rate moorings separately or to rate several moorings as one hereditament.

Rating (Exemption of Unoccupied Industrial and Storage Hereditaments) Regulations 1985

Amends Sched 1 of the GRA 1967 in that from 1 April 1985 local authorities' powers to levy rates on empty warehouse property are suspended.

Paying for Local Government (published January 1986)

Government White Paper proposing:

(a) abolition of domestic rates, to be replaced by a 'community charge' poll tax;
(b) revaluation of all non-domestic hereditaments, list to take effect from 1 April 1990;
(c) simplification of grant system to local authorities.

Queen's speech (12 November 1986)

Proposal for the introduction of the provisions of 'Paying for Local Government' into Scotland within the forthcoming parliamentary session, as a prelude to its introduction into England and Wales.

Appendix 2

Criticisms of the rating system

The rating system has been under review for decades, but the urgent need for some positive action to respond to criticisms has been relatively recent.

Since the committee of inquiry's 1976 Report on Local Government Finance (the Layfield Report), the government has indicated its changing views and perception of the rating system in 'Local Government Finance' (White Paper published in 1977); 'Alternatives to Domestic Rates' (Green Paper published in 1981); 'Rates—Proposals for Rate Limitation and Reform of the Rating System' (White Paper published in 1983); and 'Paying for Local Government' (Green Paper, published in 1986).

These government publications, together with informed opinion as published in many specialist professional journals, should be referred to for detailed criticisms of and support for the rating system, and for explanations and justification of, and possible solutions to, the problems. (A list of selected references is included at the end of this Appendix.)

Before itemising the criticisms, it should be remembered that rates (like any other tax) can be looked at from different points of view, each equally valid (see Local Taxation—A Preliminary Checklist for Layfield by C Stuart Page). Thus, a disadvantage from the point of view of the taxpayer may be an advantage from the point of view of the tax collector.

There follow some of the most commonly voiced criticisms of the present rating system with, where appropriate, justifications or explanations of any misconception.

1 Accountability

It is often considered essential for the local authorities who spend the revenue raised to be clearly and directly accountable to the taxpayers, if local money is to be spent wisely.

The size of central government grants to local authorities; the degree of control which central government exerts over local authority services; the fact that local authorities are directly answerable to the local electorate, not all of whom are ratepayers; and the fact that local authorities receive income from ratepayers who may not be among the electorate all serve to distort and obscure local accountability.

172

2 Ability to pay

Rates are not directly linked to the ability to pay of the taxpayer. However, there is generally reckoned to be an element of choice in the accommodation a ratepayer occupies, which is usually broadly linked to his financial status.

3 Arbitrary and unfair exemptions and reliefs

Such an accusation can be levied against the historically justifiable exemption given to *agricultural land and buildings*. Properties occupied by *charities* could gain rate relief direct from central government funds. In other words, charities should pay rates normally, but claim back the amount of those rates from central government funds, so that the relief from rates is supported directly by national taxation.

Properties valued on a *statutory formula*, or for which a contribution is made in lieu of rates, should pay rates on a basis which is seen to be as open and objective as for any other ratepayers. (Equality should be *seen* to be achieved in taxation.) By widening the tax base to include the occupiers of such properties, some of the *perceived inequalities* would be eliminated.

4 Failure to maintain regular revaluations

The rating system provided for five-yearly revaluations (until 1980) but quinquennial revaluations were never achieved. Central government interference (for whatever reason) has produced a tax base which is today fourteen years out of date. The relativity of the current tax liability is, therefore, based on the regional and economic value relativities of the early 1970s and, quite apart from the inequality of that fact, any changes in those relativities which results from a future revaluation is going to cause sudden and, in some cases, drastic changes in tax liabilities.

5 Delays in appeals procedure

It has been proposed to limit the right of a ratepayer to appeal against his assessment only during the first year of a valuation list, and to occasions where there has been a material change of circumstances affecting the value or a change of occupier. Appeals to the Lands Tribunal should be limited to cases involving points of law, precedent or special circumstances, such as cases of great magnitude or complexity.

The cheap, easy and relatively straightforward appeals procedure in rating is considered a great advantage to the ratepayer, especially when compared with appeals procedures in other taxes.

6 Rates are perceptible

This means that rates are paid directly by the ratepayer out of cash in hand, a very obvious and large expenditure (especially when paid at six-monthly intervals). This can be contrasted with payments of income tax which, when deducted at source, are imperceptible, and therefore focus little attention on the amount of income tax paid and how it is spent, increased, administered, etc.

The ratepayer tends to be more aware of the amount of rates he pays than of any income tax or national insurance which may be deducted at source.

The perceptibility of rates may be considered advantageous since it raises the ratepayers' level of awareness of the local authority services for which rates are levied.

Perceptibility is, however, considered to be an old-fashioned characteristic of any form of expenditure, in a society moving rapidly to direct bank account debits from plastic cards.

7 Ignorance of the basic system

Ratepayers are generally ignorant about the basic system of rate administration and rate calculation. The Layfield Report discovered, for example, that over half the country's adults have no knowledge of the basic method of calculating rates bills (ie rateable value × rate in the £).

This is not a fault of the system, but of its image and public perception. Having been in existence for so long, it perhaps assumes a familiarity which is misleading.

It is also considered that, as a tax, rates are not unpopular; in other words, ratepayers do not object to paying rates—the objection relates to the *amount* of rates which are payable.

8 Property is not a fair base for local taxation

Basing rates on the occupation of property may be considered as a tax on a necessity.

However, there is an element of personal choice exercised by residential occupiers which reflects the extent to which people choose to spend their money.

In addition, as rates are levied on local immovable assets, few rate collection problems arise for the rating authorities, and there is no problem in allocating the sums raised to individual local authority areas.

9 Rates are not wisely spent

The popular view that at least part of the proceeds of rates is squandered was a finding of the Layfield Report.

This criticism cannot be blamed on the rating system. The problem stems partly from the quality of politicians, partly from the built-in tendency of all bureaucracies to expand, and partly from a system of budgeting which, amongst other things, encourages a spending spree every February.

10 Rates are regressive

In other words, they take proportionally more income from poorer ratepayers than richer ratepayers. While statistics provided by various reports support this criticism, the regressive nature of rates has been reduced by the 'housing benefit' scheme and other methods of relief. It is also contended that the percentage of weekly expenditure paid on rates has remained relatively constant for decades.

11 Rates may be wrongly perceived as a problem

Many criticisms arise not because of the system's inherent weakness but because of outside influences, some of which affect the whole economic structure, for example:

  (a) the effect of inflation on labour-intensive local government services;
  (b) the imposition by central government of additional duties on local authorities, without granting additional income resources;
  (c) the postponement of revaluations;
  (d) the 'rate-capping' legislation, designed to secure central government's control of local authority expenditure and, thus, reduce inflation;
  (e) the conflict between a democratically elected Parliament and a democratically elected town hall.

12 Rates paid bear no relation to services enjoyed

Rates are generally perceived as a payment for local services enjoyed, and as such should be directly linked to the extent those services are enjoyed by the ratepayer.

This argument is fallacious for two reasons:

  (a) rates are a tax, not a payment for services;
  (b) rates support services, including education, which provide a quality environment from which all local residents benefit.

13 Wage-earners who are not householders do not contribute to local authority revenues

This criticism ignores the substantial share of local government income provided by national taxation, through central government grants, to which all wage-earners contribute.

14 Rates are outdated

Rates have been in operation in substantially the same form since their introduction in 1601.

However, rates, as a property tax which raises local revenue, are not 'an outdated relic of Elizabeth I'. They are used in many 'developed' countries in Europe and America (see also 15(a) below).

It does make more sense, though, for rates to be based on the prevailing system of land tenure, eg capital value for domestic property.

15 Rates are not fair

This statement can be divided into two.

    (a) Rates as a tax on the occupation of landed property are not fair, because the occupation of landed property is not a fair basis on which to levy a tax (see 8 above)

    (b) Rates as a tax are not administered fairly, ie all occupiers do not pay rates on the value of their occupations (due allowance being made for cases of hardship). For example, the arbitrary and historically justifiable exemptions of agricultural land, the use of statutory formulae for valuing the occupation by statutory undertakers, and the relief granted to residential occupiers who carry out minor structural alterations to their dwellings after 1 April 1974 (see 3 above).

However, all these (and other different treatments of selective occupiers or property) were introduced and incorporated within the rating system by central government, leaving local government to administer and (apparently) be blamed for an unfair system.

It can also be argued that no system of taxation is totally fair. In the Lords' debate, Viscount Ridley stated that there was no solution which was totally fair; neither would there ever be. But some form of property tax was likely to be as fair as anything else.

16 Rates are a tax levied on the disenfranchised

In every other case of tax payment, except corporate taxation, the taxpayer has the right to voice his concern about the level, administration etc of the tax. As far as rates are concerned, only domestic ratepayers have this fundamental right, because the commercial ratepayer is not able to vote in local council elections in his capacity as a commercial ratepayer.

It has been said that the domestic ratepayer acts as a shield for the commercial ratepayer because the level of domestic rate is controlled by the action of the electorate, who thus safeguard the interests of ratepayers who have no direct representation on local authorities.

However, domestic ratepayers are protected from the full effects of rates by the reduced rate in the pound they enjoy under s 48 of the GRA 1967. In any event, the constitutional issue of a taxpayer who has no voice in fixing the level of the tax, its spending or its administration is not solved.

17 Advantages

Despite the criticisms, rates do have several major advantages. This is why the abolition of the rating system, which it proposed in the 1970s, has been such a political problem for the Conservative government.

Rates are hard to avoid, and this results in the local authorities being very certain of their annual income, without having to waste it on bad debts. (Rates are estimated to cost 2 per cent of their yield to administer. This is low when compared with, say, development land tax which cost 6.6 per cent in 1984/85, as reported in *Rating and Valuation Reporter*, October 1984.)

A ratepayer knows the amount of his liability as soon as the rate in the pound is announced and, with the limited availability of payment by instalments, has an opportunity to spread payment over the rate period.

The system is extremely open with both the valuation list and the rate in the pound being made public, and with cheap public sources of appeal.

Rates are unique to local government, and relate directly and demonstrably to the services which local authorities provide (or fail to provide). This means that, at least in theory, the ratepayers are able to see and control (via the ballot box) the wise spending of their money (see 1 above).

Rates yield a large amount of income. As a tax, their yield is exceeded only by that of income tax. It is considered to be a stable yet buoyant yield, capable of responding quickly to required increases.

18 Conclusion

Rates cannot be considered in isolation from other taxes nor from basic principles of taxation. Similarly, local government's sources of finance cannot be considered in isolation from local government structure and expenditure.

Taxation can be regarded as the responsibility of central government in its role as the manager of the nation's economy. In this light, central government can justify some element of control over and interference in the rating system.

However, it is argued that the aims and strategies of the parties involved should be clearly stated, universally recognised and not exceeded, so that such ideals as local democracy, local accountability and control of inflation through a reduction in government expenditure are achieved—without being mutually exclusive.

19 References

Alternatives to Domestic Rates, Cmnd 8449, December 1981 (the Green Paper).

Association's Document of Additional Submissions On Layfield, Report to Department of the Environment, *Rating and Valuation*, May 1976, p 131.

Document on Rating System and Possible Alternative Sources of Revenue, *Rating and Valuation*, April 1978, p 99.

Egarr, R, Future of the Local Property Tax in Britain, *International Assessor*, July 1978, p 1.

Local Government Finance: Report of the Committee of Inquiry, Cmnd 6453, May 1976 (the Layfield Report).

Lords' debate on the rating system (10 February 1982), *Rating and Valuation*, April 1982, p 109.

Oxley, M, The Future of Rating, 240 EG 529.

Page, C S, Local Taxation—A Preliminary Checklist for Layfield, *Rating and Valuation*, June 1976, p 163.

Page, C S, Rates—The Right Tax for Local Government, *Rating and Valuation*, October 1980, p 229.

Paying for Local Government, Cmnd 9714, January 1986 (the Green Paper).

Rates—Proposals for Rate Limitation and Reform of the Rating System, Cmnd 9008, August 1983 (the White Paper).

Tinsley, C H, Rating—The Way Ahead, 239 EG 962.

Valuation Aspects of the Layfield Report, 240 EG 445.

What the Green Paper Missed, *Public Service and Local Government*, February 1982, p 9.

Appendix 3

The future of the rating system

Since the publication of the Layfield Report on Local Finance in May 1976, there has been speculation on how the rating system was to be reformed.

The widespread and, in some cases, fundamental criticisms of the rating system (see Appendix 2) made the continuation of the system in the format documented in this book almost impossible.

Mrs Thatcher's declaration in the 1970s of her intention to abolish domestic rates, and the succession of government papers on the future of rates culminating in the Green Paper 'Paying for Local Government' in January 1986, have shown that political recognition of the need to reform the rate system exists.

However, rates as a system cannot be considered in isolation from rates as a tax, as a source of income for local authorities over which central government had (prior to the Rates Act 1984) no direct control, nor from the general economic policy which any government intends to implement.

Public and economic pressures shape the political view which will ultimately make the decision on the future of the rating system.

Since the publication in January 1986 of 'Paying for Local Government', and the government's policy—declared in the Queen's speech on 12 November 1986—of implementing its proposals, it is possible to outline the *present government's intentions* regarding the future of rating.

There is likely to be a *revaluation of all non-domestic hereditaments*, the valuation list taking effect on 1 April 1990. (All such hereditaments will be valued direct to net annual value following the provisions of the LGPLA 1980.)

Regular *revaluations*, either quinquennial or 'rolling', eg one-fifth of all non-domestic properties revalued each year, will be undertaken (although, based on past evidence, the success of such an undertaking must be viewed with suspicion).

In recognition of the lack of direct control which commercial ratepayers have over the policies of local authorities, there will be a *uniform business rate* (UBR) fixed by central government and indexed to allow for inflation.

The total sums collected are to be *pooled and redistributed* to authorities on a per capita basis, each authority keeping the sums which it collects to which it is entitled, and either passing on any surplus to the Department of the

Environment (or Welsh Office) or receiving additional funds from the relevant government department.

In order to encourage local authorities to promote the development of their rateable value base and to have productive dialogue with local employers, they will retain the discretion to levy a small rate (say five per cent of the national UBR) on their non-domestic rate base, and to retain all the proceeds.

These reforms will:

(a) Introduce a radical simplification of the grant arrangements and narrow the gap between those who vote for and those who pay for local services.

(b) Offer certainty about future increases in non-domestic rates and an ending of the arbitrary variations in the sum demanded of non-domestic ratepayers. This should aid those making investment decisions to plan with greater confidence. The commitment to regular or rolling revaluations should ensure that non-domestic rates are levied on as fair a basis as possible.

(c) Allow local authorities to continue collectively to enjoy the full benefits of the non-domestic rate, but 'it will no longer be open to individual authorities to ask businesses in their area to fund excessive spending' (The Green Paper, p 18, paras 2.45–7).

Using the three main tests a local tax should satisfy—technical adequacy, fairness and promotion of local democratic accountability (The Green Paper, p 19)—the government has decided to *abolish domestic rates*.

In its place there is to be a poll tax, called the *community charge*—a new flat-rate charge payable by all adult residents within a local authority area.

The level of the community charge will be *fixed by local authorities* and levied on all local adult residents. There will continue to be some assistance for people on low income.

The *problems of enforcing* the community charge are considered to be 'not insurmountable'.

A register of all adults living in the area will be compiled based on local authority records, the electoral register, use of local services, and information provided by 'the head of the household'. The possibility of evading the community charge by failing to register will be reduced by making the head of the household liable to criminal sanctions should he fail to provide information for the register.

Transitional arrangements would be made during the change-over from domestic rates to community charge, and there are special provisions relating to occupiers of Crown property, students and second-home owners.

In this way, the government intends to improve local accountability by widening the tax base, ie by making all local authority voters local authority taxpayers. This should:

(a) provide a clear link between local spending decisions and local tax bills; and

(b) by spreading the burden of local taxation to all adults, improve the relationship between the use of and payment for services. All local electors would have a clear incentive to consider the costs as well as the benefits of extra local spending (the Green Paper, p 27, paras 3.47–8).

In addition to the proposals for non-domestic and domestic properties, the Green Paper outlines the government's intention to *reform the system of central government grants*.

The intention is to compensate for real differences in local authorities' needs and to provide additional help in the form of a flat-rate sum per adult.

No information has been given in this text about what the central government grant comprises and how it operates—such information being considered to be beyond its scope. However, a brief outline of the proposals contained in the Green Paper is relevant in relation to the future of the rating system as part of the sources of income for local government.

Central government grants provide local authorities with income in order to:

(a) *equalise the needs* of different authorities, eg by reflecting the greater need for education in one area because of the high number of children of school age, as compared with an area with a low number of such children;

(b) *equalise the resources* between areas with a low rateable value per capita as compared with an area with a high rateable value per capita; and

(c) recognise the fact that certain services provided by local authorities have a wider *national dimension* (such as education) and, since rates are not based on ability to pay, they should not bear the full weight of local authority expenditure.

A new grants system should be simple to operate, easily understood, be stable and certain in yield, and show the direct link between changes in authorities' spending and changes in local tax bills.

In order to achieve these aims the government proposes a grant system on a per capita basis comprising:

(a) needs grant, to compensate authorities for differences in the cost of providing a standard level of service to meet local needs;

(b) standard grant, to provide an additional contribution from national taxation towards the cost of local services.

In order to achieve a system where the tax bill could be the same in different parts of the country for a given standard level of service, there will be transitional arrangements to avoid the sudden and substantial shifts in the burden of local domestic taxation between areas.

The Green Paper envisages the introduction of similar provisions in Scotland, and these were proposed within the 1986/87 parliamentary sitting in the Queen's speech delivered on 12 November 1986.

The Scottish reform is viewed as a prelude to the introduction of the proposed system for England and Wales (although there are differences to the proposed system in Wales), and the fact that such reforms could be on the statute book in 1987 shows that the political will of the present government has at last been converted to parliamentary action.

Appendix 4

Documents used in rating

1 Aggrieved person's proposal form
2 Valuation officer's proposal form to include a new hereditament into the valuation list
3 Valuation officer's proposal form to alter an existing entry in the valuation list
4 Copy of letter accompanying the valuation officer's objection
5 Agreement forms
6 Valuation officer's explanation of procedure, sent as an acknowledgement of receipt of an aggrieved person's proposal
7 Page from the valuation list, Section I
8 Page from the valuation list, Section II, direction sheets
9 Page from the valuation list, Section III, totals
10 Rent return (GRA 1967, s 82)

Documents used in rating

1

GENERAL RATE ACT 1967

PROPOSAL FOR ALTERATION OF VALUATION LIST

ADDRESS OF PROPERTY to which this proposal relates (including postcode if known):

Office No

This proposal must be sent to the Valuation Officer at:

where any assistance required in completing this form may readily be obtained on request.

RATING AREA: RATING DISTRICT:

*Name of the person or body by whom or on whose behalf the proposal is made:

Alteration which that person or body proposes should be made in the valuation list:

Ground on which that alteration is proposed:

*Name of occupier: *Name of owner:

Dated: _____

Capacity in which signed: _____

Signed: _____

Telephone No.:

(e.g. as occupier, owner, agent for occupier, agent for owner, etc.)

*Name and address of person to whom communications are to be sent if address differs from the address of the property;

*IN BLOCK LETTERS

FOR USE IN THE VALUATION OFFICE ONLY

ASSESSMENT NO. _____ ANALYSIS CODE _____

DESCRIPTION _____

ADDRESS _____

G.V.£ _____ N.A.V.£ _____ R.V.£ _____

DATE RECEIVED _____ DATE ACKNOWLEDGED _____

GENERAL RATE ACT 1967

SECTION 69(1).

Subject to subsection (6) of this section, any person (including a rating authority) who is aggrieved—

(a) by the inclusion of any hereditament in the valuation list; or

(b) by any value ascribed in the list to a hereditament or by any other statement made or omitted to be made in the list with respect to a hereditament; or

(c) in the case of a building or portion of a building occupied in parts, by the valuation in the list of that building or portion of a building as a single hereditament,

may at any time make a proposal for the alteration of the list so far as it relates to that hereditament.

SECTION 69(3).

Without prejudice to any right exercisable by rating authorities by virtue of subsection (1) of this section, where—

(a) it appears to a rating authority that a hereditament in their rating area which is not included in the list ought to be included therein; and

(b) the valuation officer gives notice in writing to the rating authority that he does not intend to make a proposal for inserting that hereditament in the list,

the rating authority, at any time within twenty-eight days after the date on which that notice was given, may make a proposal for the alteration of the list by the insertion of that hereditament therein.

SECTION 69(4)

Where a proposal in relation to a hereditament has been made under the foregoing provisions of this section, a further proposal for the alteration of the list in relation to that hereditament may be so made which is contingent on an alteration being made in consequence of the earlier proposal.

SECTION 69(5).

Every proposal under this section must—

(a) be made in writing; and

(b) specify the grounds on which the proposed alteration is supported; and

(c) comply with any requirements of any regulations made by the Minister with respect to the form of such proposals and otherwise with respect to the making thereof, and every such proposal made otherwise than by the valuation officer must be served on tne valuation officer.

2

VALUATION OFFICER'S ADDRESS

GENERAL RATE ACT 1967

PROPOSAL FOR ALTERATION OF VALUATION LIST

RATING AREA

RATING DISTRICT

I hereby make a proposal for the alteration of the Valuation List for the above-named Rating Area by the inclusion in the List of the entry shown below. The hereditament to which the said entry relates is not now included in the said Valuation List.

VALUATION AREA

DATE

VALUATION OFFICER

ASSESSMENT NUMBER 1	ANALYSIS CODE 2	DESCRIPTION 3	ADDRESS and name of occupier or owner "O" if required for identification 4	GROSS VALUE 5	RATEABLE VALUE 6
				£	£

or Present Occupier

The Clerk to the Rating Authority

Date of Transmission of this copy:

The above is a copy of a proposal which has been made to alter the Valuation List. A statement of the right of Objection to the proposal is set out overleaf.

VO 7010 (12/85)

185

RIGHT OF OBJECTION

The owner or occupier of the whole or any part of a hereditament to which the proposal relates may object in writing to it and any such objection must reach the Valuation Officer within twenty-eight days from the date on which the copy of the proposal is served upon the occupier.

A form on which to make an objection may be obtained from the Valuation Officer.

In any correspondence please quote the assessment number (shown in Col. 1 of the proposal) and the address of the property.

The Rating Authority in certain circumstances may also object to the proposal within twenty-eight days from the date on which the copy of the proposal is served upon them.

EFFECT OF THIS PROPOSAL ON RATE LIABILITY

The date from which an alteration in the Valuation List has effect is prescribed by law. Generally, where a proposal by the Valuation Officer to alter a Valuation List results in a changed value it affects liability for rates from the beginning of the rate period current when the Notice of Proposal is served upon the occupier. There are exceptions to this general rule. Where, for example, the proposal relates to a new hereditament or to structural alterations to an existing hereditament, the alteration in the Valuation List may have effect from a date later than the beginning of the rate period.

A ratepayer who wishes to know the possible effect of this proposal on his liability for the payment of rates should consult the Rating Authority at the address shown overleaf.

3

GENERAL RATE ACT 1967

PROPOSAL FOR ALTERATION OF VALUATION LIST

VALUATION OFFICER'S ADDRESS

RATING AREA

RATING DISTRICT

I hereby make a proposal for the alteration of the Valuation List for the above-named Rating Area by the deletion of the existing entry or entries and the insertion of the proposed entry or entries shown below.

The grounds on which the proposed alteration is supported are:

VALUATION AREA

DATE

VALUATION OFFICER

ASSESSMENT NUMBER	ANALYSIS CODE	DESCRIPTION	ADDRESS and name of occupier or owner "O" if required for identification	GROSS VALUE	RATEABLE VALUE
1	2	3	4	5	6
Existing Entry or Entries				£	£
Proposed Entry or Entries					

The Clerk to the Rating Authority

or Present Occupier

Date of Transmission of this copy

The above is a copy of a proposal which has been made to alter the Valuation List.

A statement of the right of Objection to the proposal is set out overleaf.

187

RIGHT OF OBJECTION

The owner or occupier of the whole or any part of a hereditament to which the proposal relates may object in writing to it and any such objection must reach the Valuation Officer within twenty-eight days from the date on which the copy of the proposal is served upon the occupier.

A form on which to make an objection may be obtained from the Valuation Officer.

In any correspondence please quote the assessment number (shown in Col. 1 of the proposal) and the address of the property.

The Rating Authority in certain circumstances may also object to the proposal within twenty-eight days from the date on which the copy of the proposal is served upon them.

EFFECT OF THIS PROPOSAL ON RATE LIABILITY

The date from which an alteration in the Valuation List has effect is prescribed by law. Generally, where a proposal by the Valuation Officer to alter a Valuation List results in a changed value it affects liability for rates from the beginning of the rate period current when the Notice of Proposal is served upon the occupier. There are exceptions to this general rule. Where, for example, the proposal relates to a new hereditament or to structural alterations to an existing hereditament, the alteration in the Valuation List may have effect from a date later than the beginning of the rate period.

A ratepayer who wishes to know the possible effect of this proposal on his liability for the payment of rates should consult the Rating Authority at the address shown overleaf.

4

Valuation Office
Inland Revenue

Assessment No

*Please use this reference if you write
or call. It will help avoid delay.*

From

Telephone
Ext
Date

Notification of Objection to Rating Assessment Proposal

Address:

Description in Valuation List:

I enclose a copy of an objection which has been made to the proposal made by you on
for the alteration of the Valuation List entry for the above
property.

In my acknowledgement of your proposal I explained that as soon as circumstances
permit I will make arrangements to discuss the matter with you.

Unless agreement is reached by all parties or your proposal or all objections outstanding
are withdrawn the papers will within 4 months be sent to the Clerk to the Local
Valuation Panel.

This has the effect of an appeal by you to any objection outstanding.

Notification of the date and time of the hearing will be sent to you by the Local
Valuation Panel but if you have any further queries please contact my office.

Valuation Officer

Valuation Area

5

**Valuation Office
Inland Revenue**

Agreement to alter the Valuation List

This is an agreement to alter the Valuation List in respect of the proposal dated .... **made by** ....

All persons, whose agreement is necessary under the General Rate Act 1967 Section 72, agree that the existing entry(ies) should be altered to read as shown below.

After signing where applicable this form should be returned to the Valuation Officer.

Existing entry(ies)

		Rating Area		Rating District		
Assessment Number	Analysis Code	Description	Address & Name of occupier or owner 'O' if required for identification		Gross Value £	Rateable Value £

Altered entry(ies)

Signed by or on behalf of:-

1. **The maker of the proposal** ....
   being the – *Agent for/ Owner/ Occupier/ Valuation Officer/ Rating Authority/ other

2. **The occupier** ....
   If not already signed at 1 above.

3. **The owner** ....
   If not already signed at 1 or 2 and then only necessary if owner has objected to the proposal or is required, or has agreed with the Rating Authority, to pay the rates.

   *Delete those not applicable

4. **The Rating Authority** ....
   (if required)

5. **The Valuation Officer** ....

   Date: ....
   (To be completed by Valuation Officer)

Schedule forming part of agreement to alter the Valuation List

Proposal dated   Made by

Rating Area   Rating District

Assessment Number	Analysis Code	Description	Address & Name of occupier or owner "O" if required for identification	Gross Value £	Rateable Value £

6

**Valuation Office
Inland Revenue**

From:

Telephone: Ext:

Rating Assessment

Date:

Dear Sir/Madam

Address of Property:

Proposal received on:

I acknowledge receipt of your proposal concerning the above property. A copy is being sent to any person having the right to object to it.

I will be giving consideration to your proposal as soon as possible and, if necessary, I will arrange to inspect the property. But as proposals are usually dealt with in date order, it may be a little while before I am ready to contact you.

If I find that I can give effect to your proposal, and there has been no objection to it or any objection has been withdrawn, I will let you know in due course. However, if the matter is not settled within four months of the date I received your proposal, it will be necessary for me to inform the Clerk to the Local Valuation Panel.

This will have effect as an appeal by you to the Local Valuation Court as explained in the notice on the back of this letter.

If the appeal cannot be resolved and a Court hearing becomes necessary, the date, time and place of the hearing will be sent to you by the Clerk to the Panel. You will then be able to attend the hearing and state your case.

On the other hand, if, after further consideration and/or discussion:—

    a.   we are able to settle your proposal by agreement; or
    b.   you decide to withdraw your proposal,

it will not be necessary for the appeal to proceed to a hearing by the Local Valuation Court.

Please note that if you pay the rates on the property and wish to make any enquiry about the amount you pay, or the method of payment, you should contact the Rates Department at your local council offices.

If you have any other queries concerning the rating valuation of the property, or the procedure for dealing with your proposal, please contact my office quoting the assessment number shown above.

Yours Faithfully

Valuation Officer

Please turn over

**Notice to Maker of proposal as required by section 74(4)
of the General Rate Act 1967**

If the Valuation Officer has not notified the maker of a proposal within a period of four months beginning with the date on which the proposal was served on him, that he is satisfied the proposal is "well-founded", and the proposal is not withdrawn, the Valuation Officer shall send to the Clerk to the Local Valuation Panel:—

    a.   a copy of the proposal;

    b.   a statement that the Valuation Officer objects to the proposal; and

    c.   a copy of any notice of objection to the proposal served on the Valuation Officer which has not been unconditionally withdrawn.

The Valuation Officer will not be able to treat a proposal as "well-founded" if a notice of objection against the proposal has been served on him within the time allowed unless that notice of objection is unconditionally withdrawn.

Where the Valuation Officer sends a copy of a proposal to the Clerk to the Local Valuation Panel, this will have effect as an appeal to the Local Valuation Court, by the person who made the proposal, against the objection by the Valuation Officer and any objection made by any other person.

A proposal can be settled if all parties agree on an alteration of the valuation list (whether the alteration is that specified in the proposal or another alteration).

Such an agreement can be made at any time before a copy of the proposal is sent to the Clerk to the Local Valuation Panel or after that time provided the Local Valuation Court has not given a decision.

7

RATING AREA   RATING DISTRICT   SECTION 1   PAGE No.

ASSESSMENT No. 1	ANALYSIS CODE 2	DESCRIPTION 3	ADDRESS (& NAME OF OCCUPIER, OR OWNER, "O" IF REQUIRED FOR IDENTIFICATION) 4	GROSS VALUE 5 £	RATEABLE VALUE 6 £	REFERENCE NO. OF AMENDMENT 7

TOTAL £

8

RATING AREA   RATING DISTRICT   SECTION II DIRECTION SHEET No. D

DIRECT NO.	ASSESSMENT NO. 1	ANALYSIS CODE 2	DESCRIPTION 3	ADDRESS & NAME OF OCCUPIER, OR OWNER "O", IF REQUIRED FOR IDENTIFICATION 4	GROSS VALUE 5 £	RATEABLE VALUE 6 £	RATEABLE VALUE LAST SHOWN IN VALUATION LIST 6 £	REF. NO. OF AMENDMT 7

TOTALS £   £

NET ADDITIONS TO TOTALS £   NET DED'NS FROM TOTALS £

VO 7191 (7/85)   Printed in the UK for HMSO Dd 8891845 3M Pads 10/85 JCM 722237/0

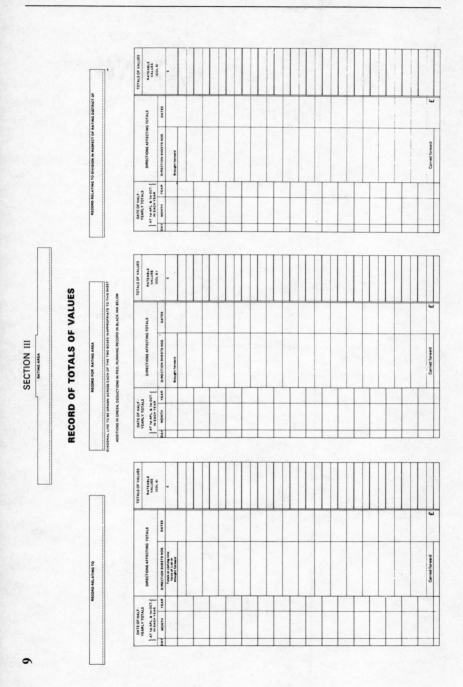

SECTION III

RATING AREA

RECORD OF TOTALS OF VALUES

10

Notice requiring
a return for

RATING

General Rate Act
1967

Rating Area

Rating District

Reference no.

Date

Telephone no.   Extension

or Present Occupier

Valuation Officer's address

**Property
address**

You are required under Section 82 of the General Rate Act 1967 to complete this form in respect of the above mentioned property and, having signed the **declaration**, return it to me **within 21 days** using the enclosed envelope/label.

The information you give is for my use in making or objecting to a proposal to alter the current valuation list.

If there is not enough space for any of your answers please continue on a separate sheet of paper. Any separate papers should show the question number and be attached to this form.

Should you need any help in completing the form please let me know.

VALUATION OFFICER

Documents used in rating

Please print in BLOCK CAPITALS and circle the appropriate answer eg **yes** /**no**

1 Details of property

1·1 Address _____

post
code

2 Occupier

2·1 Name of present occupier _____

2·2 Date present occupier first occupied the property _____

3 Owner

3·1 Name and address of your immediate landlord or the person to whom rent is paid (see note 3·1)

_____

_____

4 Description

4·1 Purpose for which the property is used at present (see note 4·1) _____

4·2 Nature of trade or business (eg greengrocers, solicitors, bakery etc) _____

5 Rent

5.1 What is the amount of rent now payable by the occupier? (see note 5.1) £_____ per _____

5.2 Does the rent at 5.1 include a ground rent? **yes/no**   If **yes** £_____ per _____

5.3 Is the rent now payable for the whole property: **yes/no**

If **no**, describe that part to which it relates. Indicate the
location of floors or rooms, eg ground floor only, two rooms first floor (front) _____

5.4 Does the rent now payable include
general rates   water rates   other rates (see note 5.4). If **yes,** give details _____
yes/no   **yes/no**   **yes/no**

5.5 Who is responsible for payment of (see note 5.5)
outside repairs   inside repairs   insurance of property
tenant/landlord   **tenant/landlord**   **tenant/landlord**

If any of these payments are shared give details _____

5.6 Give the date the rent at 5.1 first became payable. Disregard any date when
the rent was altered due solely to a change in the amount of rates payable _____

5.7 If the rent now payable is subject to variation give
review dates and revised rents where fixed (see note 5.7) _____

5.8 Does the rent now payable **include** a sum for any services provided by the landlord? (see note 5.8) **yes/no**

amount included in the
If **yes**, give details _____ rent for them (if known) £ _____

5.9 Is a **separate** payment made to the landlord for any services? (see notes 5.9 and 5.1) **yes/no**

If **yes**, give details _____ amount £ _____ per _____

Please read these notes

3.1
**If owner/occupied enter
'as occupier' then
complete questions 4, 8
(if applicable) and the
Declaration**

4·1
Eg shop, shop with living
accommodation, office,
factory, sports ground etc

5.1
Week, calendar month,
quarter, year etc.

5.4
'Other rates' refers to such
items as general service
charge or sewerage rate etc

5.5
If the **landlord** pays but
recovers the cost from the
tenant the answer should be
tenant. If the **tenant** pays
but recovers the cost from
the **landlord** the answer
should be **landlord**

5.7
Refers to rents which can be
varied, under the lease or
agreement, at stipulated
intervals or for specific
reasons such as fluctuations
in trade or takings but **not** to
variations due to the amount
of rates payable

5.8, 5.9
Lighting, heating, cleaning
etc of the property or of the
parts shared with other
tenants

5.10 Does the rent now payable include a sum for the use of any trade fixtures, fittings, plant and machinery, furniture or other equipment? **yes/no**

If **yes**, give details and amount agreed _____ £ _____

5.11 Does the rent now payable include a specific sum for the use of parking space and/or garaging? **yes/no**

If **yes**, give the number of spaces and/or garages _____ and amount included £ _____

6 Alterations and improvements

6.1 Have any alterations, additions or improvements been made,
or are any to be made, by the occupier **as a condition** of the present tenancy? (see note 6·1)   **yes / no**

If **yes**, give details. _____

cost £ _____ date completed. _____

Are these to be reflected in the revised rent at any review date? (see 5·6)   **yes / no**

6.2 Have any alterations, additions or improvements been made **other than as a condition** of the present tenancy? (see note 6·2)   **yes / no**

If **yes**, give details. _____

cost £ _____ date completed. _____

6·1, 6·2
If the works are not yet completed indicate the likely date of completion and the estimated final cost

7 Lease or agreement

7·1 On what date did the present lease or agreement commence? _____

7·2 For how many years was the lease or agreement granted? _____

7·3 Can it be terminated by either the landlord or the tenant?   **yes / no**

If **yes**, when and in what circumstances. _____

7·4 Does the lease or agreement contain any special conditions?   **yes / no**

If **yes**, give details. _____

7·5 Did the occupier pay additional money as a premium
to the landlord for the granting of the lease or agreement?   **yes/no**   If **yes**, state the amount £ _____

7·6 Did the occupier purchase the lease or agreement?   **yes / no**   If **yes**, give the amount of consideration paid £ _____

Did the consideration include a sum for goodwill, fixtures and fittings?   **yes / no**

If **yes**, the amount paid for each item _____ date of payment _____

7·7 Was a former lease or agreement surrendered as a condition of the granting of the present lease or agreement?   **yes / no**

If **yes**, state the amount of rent payable under the surrendered lease or agreement   £ _____ per annum

Term unexpired at
date of surrender_____ years.

7·8 Is the present lease or agreement a renewal of a former tenancy held by the present occupier?   **yes / no**

If **yes**, state if the amount of the new rent was determined by the County Court under the Landlord and Tenant Act 1954   **yes / no**

At the time the rent was agreed between landlord and tenant, or determined by order
of the County Court, what alterations, additions or improvements, if any, were disregarded? _____

Documents used in rating

8 Lettings

8·1 Does the occupier named in 2·1 receive any rent from letting any part or parts of the property (including advertising rights, stations or hoardings) ? **yes / no**

If **yes,** answer the following

Part let	Name of tenant and address if not resident at the property	Rent received per year £	Year rent fixed	Does the rent payable include general and other rates ?
		£	19	**yes / no**
		£	19	**yes / no**
		£	19	**yes / no**
		£	19	**yes / no**
		£	19	**yes / no**
		£	19	**yes / no**

Declaration
To be signed and completed by the person making this return.
False statements or failure to complete this return can result in prosecution.

To the best of my knowledge and belief the particulars given on this form are correct and complete.

Signature _____ occupier / owner / lessee

Date _____ 19_____

Address (if different from property address)

_____

_____

For valuation officer use

r.cd. _____

an.sh. _____

l.h.r. _____

c.r.t. _____

r.sh. _____

Index

201